BEING PEACE

BEING PEACE

Thich Nhat Hanh

Edited by Arnold Kotler
With illustrations by Mayumi Oda

Parallax Press
Berkeley, California

Parallax Press
P.O. Box 7355
Berkeley, California 94707
www.parallax.org

Parallax Press is the publishing division of Unified Buddhist Church, Inc.

Library of Congress Cataloging-in-Publication Data
Nhât Hanh, Thích
    Being Peace
    Collection of talks given during visit to U.S. in fall of 1985.
    1. Religious life (Buddhism)
    I. Kotler, Arnold, 1946 –   II. Title
BQ5410.N45 1987   294.3'444   87-2340
ISBN 0-938077-00-7

25 26 27 28 29 30 / 09 08 07 06 05 04

Contents

Editor's Preface

Thich Nhat Hanh was born in central Vietnam in the mid-1920's, and in 1942, at the age of sixteen, he entered the monkhood. When war came to his country, Nhat Hanh and many of his fellow monks left their monastic isolation and became actively engaged in helping victims of the war and in publicly communicating their desire for peace. In 1966, he was invited by the Fellowship of Reconciliation to tour the United States "to describe to [us] the aspirations and the agony of the voiceless masses of the Vietnamese people." He met with hundreds of groups and individuals, including Secretary of Defense McNamara, Dr. Martin Luther King, Jr., Thomas Merton, and, in Europe, Pope Paul VI. As a result of his outspoken frankness, he was unable to return to Vietnam, threatened with arrest.

After the war ended, Nhat Hanh and his colleagues on the Vietnamese Buddhist Peace Delegation in Paris tried to find legal ways to send funds to Vietnam to help feed hungry children, but they were without success. The following year, the group went to Malaysia and Singapore to try to help insure the safety of boat people on the turbulent Gulf of Siam, but various governments thwarted those efforts as well. Uncertain how to proceed, Thich Nhat Hanh entered a period of retreat, and for more than five years he remained at his hermitage in France, meditating, writing, gardening, and occasionally seeing visitors. In 1982, he accepted an invitation to the Reverence for Life Conference in New York, and I was fortunate enough to attend that conference and meet him. Soft, slow-moving, and deeply penetrating, Nhat Hanh was described by fellow conference participant Richard Baker-roshi, as "a cross between a cloud, a snail, and a piece of heavy machinery—a true religious presence."

During that trip, Nhat Hanh became aware of the tremendous interest in Buddhist meditation among Americans, and he agreed to return the following year to lead retreats on Buddhism and peace work. A monk for more than forty years, he taught two generations of novices in Vietnam, developing the skill of expressing the deepest teachings of Buddhism in straightforward, yet poetic language. Because of his experience with the war and his willingness to face the realities of our time, his teachings are also about suffering, reconciliation, and peace.

Since those visits to North America, Nhat Hanh has returned annually. *Being Peace* is a collection of

the talks he gave to peaceworkers and meditation
students during his tour of Buddhist centers in the
Fall of 1985. Most of these lectures were delivered to
groups of retreatants who were together for several
days practicing sitting and walking meditation, eating meals silently, and discussing how to create a
more peaceful world. Nhat Hanh invited the children
present to sit in front of him for the first twenty or
thirty minutes of each lecture, and you may notice
passages where he is speaking to children, although
he is also addressing the adults through them.

*   *   *

The idea of this book arose during the tour, when
several of us saw how deeply Nhat Hanh's words, in
fact his entire presence, affected and penetrated his
listeners. Thich Nhat Hanh's teachings provide a crucial antidote to our busy lives and to our anthro-
pocentric way of perceiving. It has been a great pleasure to edit this volume, to make these teachings
more widely available.

Many people helped create *Being Peace*, more than
can be acknowledged here. I especially want to thank
the Buddhist Peace Fellowship, for organizing the
tour during which these talks were given; the
Providence Zen Center, Rocky Mountain Dharma
Center, Dharma Sangha, Ojai Foundation, Sonoma
Mountain Zen Center, Green Gulch Zen Center, and
Diamond Sangha for hosting these retreats; and
Mayumi Oda, whose inspiration from meeting Nhat

Hanh at Green Gulch gave birth to the illustrations for this book. I also want to thank the many friends of Nancy Wilson Ross, including Paul and Rachel Mellon, Mary Burke, Julius and Cleome Wadsworth, Margot Wilkie, John Bailes, Yvonne Rand, and Bill Sterling, whose generosity allowed work on this book to begin; Tyrone Cashman and Marlow and Cynthia Hotchkiss, whose support as we approached the crucial final stages made completion and publication possible; Carole Melkonian, Trish Farah, Don Stoddard, Sam Rose, and the other transcribers; Gay Reineck, for many hours overseeing the book's production; Jordan Thorn, Therese Fitzgerald, Andy Cooper, Dan Asimov, Paul Rosenblum, Ruth Klein, Tony Husch, Linda Foust, Vanja Palmers, Alan Brilliant, Jack Shoemaker, Brit Pyland, Toinette Lippe, Jean Weininger, Michael Phillips, Randall Goodall, Nelson Foster, Ananda Dalenberg, Gregory Wood, John and Margo Steiner, Rose Kotler, and the many others whose unfailing help have made Parallax Press a reality; and Cao Ngoc Phuong, whose selfless work—feeding hungry children, taking care of Plum Village, and looking after all the details that make Thich Nhat Hanh's work so effective—totally embodies the teachings of understanding and love that are the foundation of "being peace."

Arnold Kotler
Berkeley, California
January 1987

BEING PEACE

If we are peaceful, if we are happy,
we can blossom like a flower,
and everyone in our family,
our entire society,
will benefit from our peace.

Suffering Is Not Enough

*L*ife is filled with suffering, but it is also filled with
many wonders, like the blue sky, the sunshine, the
eyes of a baby. To suffer is not enough. We must also
be in touch with the wonders of life. They are within
us and all around us, everywhere, any time.

If we are not happy, if we are not peaceful, we cannot share peace and happiness with others, even those
we love, those who live under the same roof. If we are
peaceful, if we are happy, we can smile and blossom
like a flower, and everyone in our family, our entire
society, will benefit from our peace. Do we need to
make a special effort to enjoy the beauty of the blue
sky? Do we have to practice to be able to enjoy it? No,
we just enjoy it. Each second, each minute of our lives
can be like this. Wherever we are, any time, we have
the capacity to enjoy the sunshine, the presence of each

other, even the sensation of our breathing. We don't need to go to China to enjoy the blue sky. We don't have to travel into the future to enjoy our breathing. We can be in touch with these things right now. It would be a pity if we were only aware of suffering.

We are so busy we hardly have time to look at the people we love, even in our own household, and to look at ourselves. Society is organized in a way that even when we have some leisure time, we don't know how to use it to get back in touch with ourselves. We have millions of ways to lose this precious time—we turn on the TV or pick up the telephone, or start the car and go somewhere. We are not used to being with ourselves, and we act as if we don't like ourselves and are trying to escape from ourselves.

Meditation is to be aware of what is going on—in our bodies, in our feelings, in our minds, and in the world. Each day 40,000 children die of hunger. The superpowers now have more than 50,000 nuclear warheads, enough to destroy our planet many times. Yet the sunrise is beautiful, and the rose that bloomed this morning along the wall is a miracle. Life is both dreadful and wonderful. To practice meditation is to be in touch with both aspects. Please do not think we must be solemn in order to meditate. In fact, to meditate well, we have to smile a lot.

Recently I was sitting with a group of children, and a boy named Tim was smiling beautifully. I said, "Tim, you have a very beautiful smile," and he said, "Thank you." I told him, "You don't have to thank me, I have to thank you. Because of your smile, you make life more beautiful. Instead of saying, 'Thank you,' you should say, 'You're welcome.'"

If a child smiles, if an adult smiles, that is very important. If in our daily life we can smile, if we can be peaceful and happy, not only we, but everyone will profit from it. This is the most basic kind of peace work. When I see Tim smiling, I am so happy. If he is aware that he is making other people happy, he can say, "You are welcome."

*   *   *

From time to time, to remind ourselves to relax, to be peaceful, we may wish to set aside some time for a retreat, a day of mindfulness, when we can walk slowly, smile, drink tea with a friend, enjoy being together as if we are the happiest people on Earth. This is not a retreat, it is a treat. During walking meditation, during kitchen and garden work, during sitting meditation, all day long, we can practice smiling. At first you may find it difficult to smile, and we have to think about why. Smiling means that we are ourselves, that we have sovereignty over ourselves, that we are not drowned into forgetfulness. This kind of smile can be seen on the faces of Buddhas and bodhisattvas.

I would like to offer one short poem you can recite from time to time, while breathing and smiling.

Breathing in, I calm my body.
Breathing out, I smile.
Dwelling in the present moment
I know this a wonderful moment.

"Breathing in, I calm my body." This line is like drinking a glass of ice water—you feel the cold, the freshness, permeate your body. When I breathe in and recite this line, I actually feel the breathing calming my body, calming my mind.

"Breathing out, I smile." You know the effect of a smile. A smile can relax hundreds of muscles in your face, and relax your nervous system. A smile makes you master of yourself. That is why the Buddhas and bodhisattvas are always smiling. When you smile, you realize the wonder of the smile.

"Dwelling in the present moment." While I sit here, I don't think of somewhere else, of the future or the past. I sit here, and I know where I am. This is very important. We tend to be alive in the future, not now. We say, "Wait until I finish school and get my Ph.D. degree, and then I will be *really* alive." When we have it, and it's not easy to get, we say to ourselves, "I have to wait until I have a job in order to be really alive." And then after the job, a car. After the car, a house. We are not capable of being alive in the present moment. We tend to postpone being alive to the future, the distant future, we don't know when. Now is not the moment to be alive. We may never be alive at all in our entire life. Therefore, the technique, if we have to speak of a technique, is to be in the present moment, to be aware that we are here and now, and the only moment to be alive is the present moment.

"I know this is a wonderful moment." This is the only moment that is real. To be here and now, and enjoy the present moment is our most important task. "Calming, Smiling, Present moment, Wonderful moment." I hope you will try it.

*   *   *

Even though life is hard, even though it is sometimes difficult to smile, we have to try. Just as when we wish each other "Good morning," it must be a real "Good morning." Recently, one friend asked me, "How can I force myself to smile when I am filled with sorrow? It isn't natural." I told her she must be able to smile to her sorrow, because we are more than our sorrow. A human being is like a television set with millions of channels. If we turn the Buddha on, we are the Buddha. If we turn sorrow on, we are sorrow. If we turn a smile on, we really are the smile. We cannot let just one channel dominate us. We have the seed of everything in us, and we have to seize the situation in our hand, to recover our own sovereignty.

When we sit down peacefully, breathing and smiling, with awareness, we are our true selves, we have sovereignty over ourselves. When we open ourselves up to a TV program, we let ourselves be invaded by the program. Sometimes it is a good program, but often it is just noisy. Because we want to have something other than ourselves enter us, we sit there and let a noisy television program invade us, assail us, destroy us. Even if our nervous system suffers, we don't have the courage to stand up and turn it off, because if we do that, we will have to return to our self.

Meditation is the opposite. It helps us return to our true self. Practicing meditation in this kind of society is very difficult. Everything seems to work in concert to try to take us away from our true self. We have thousands of things, like videotapes and music, which help us be away from ourselves. Practicing meditation is to be aware, to smile, to breathe. These are on the opposite side. We go back to ourselves in order to see what is going on, because to meditate means to be aware of what is going on. What is going on is very important.

*   *   *

Suppose you are expecting a child. You need to breathe and smile for him or her. Please don't wait until your baby is born before beginning to take care of him or her. You can take care of your baby right now, or even sooner. If you cannot smile, that is very serious. You might think, "I am too sad. Smiling is just not the correct thing to do." Maybe crying or shouting would be correct, but your baby will get it— anything you are, anything you do, is for your baby.

Even if you do not have a baby in your womb, the seed is already there. Even if you are not married, even if you are a man, you should be aware that a baby is already there, the seeds of future generations are already there. Please don't wait until the doctors tell you that you are going to have a baby to begin to take care of it. It is already there. Whatever you are, whatever you do, your baby will get it. Anything you eat, any worries that are on your mind will be for him or her. Can you tell me that you cannot smile? Think of the baby, and smile for him, for her, for the future generations. Please don't tell me that a smile and your sorrow just don't go together. It's your sorrow, but what about your baby? It's not his sorrow, it's not her sorrow.

Children understand very well that in each woman, in each man, there is a capacity of waking up, of understanding, and of loving. Many children have told me that they cannot show me anyone who does not have this capacity. Some people allow it to develop, and some do not, but everyone has it. This capacity of waking up, of being aware of what is going on in your feelings, in your body, in your perceptions, in the world, is called Buddha nature, the capacity of understanding and loving. Since the baby of that Buddha is in us, we should give him or her a chance. Smiling is very important. If we are not able to smile, then the world will not have peace. It is not by going out for a demonstration against nuclear missiles that we can bring about peace. It is with our capacity of smiling, breathing, and being peace that we can make peace.

The Three Gems

Many of us worry about the situation of the world. We don't know when the bombs will explode. We feel that we are on the edge of time. As individuals, we feel helpless, despairing. The situation is so dangerous, injustice is so widespread, the danger is so close. In this kind of situation, if we panic, things will only become worse. We need to remain calm, to see clearly. Meditation is to be aware, and to try to help.

I like to use the example of a small boat crossing the Gulf of Siam. In Vietnam, there are many people, called boat people, who leave the country in small boats. Often the boats are caught in rough seas or storms, the people may panic, and boats can sink. But if even one person aboard can remain calm, lucid, knowing what to do and what not to do, he or she can help the boat survive. His or her expression—face, voice—communicates clarity and calmness, and people have trust in that person. They will listen to what he or she says. One such person can save the lives of many.

Our world is something like a small boat. Compared with the cosmos, our planet is a very small boat. We are about to panic because our situation is no better than the situation of the small boat in the sea. You know that we have more than 50,000 nuclear weapons. Humankind has become a very dangerous species. We need people who can sit still and be able to smile, who can walk peacefully. We need people like that in order to save us. Mahayana Buddhism says that you are that person, that each of you is that person.

*   *   *

I had one student named Thich Thanh Van, who entered the monastery at the age of six, and at the age of seventeen, began to study with me. Later he was the first director of the School of Youth for Social Service, where he directed thousands of young people working during the war in Vietnam, rebuilding villages that were destroyed, and resettling tens of thousands of refugees fleeing the warzones. He was killed in an accident. I was in Copenhagen when I heard of the death of my student. He was a very gentle monk, very brave.

When he was a novice, six or seven years old, he saw people come to the temple and bring cakes and

bananas to offer to the Buddha. He wanted to know
how the Buddha eats bananas, so he waited until
everyone went home and the shrine was closed, and
then he peered through the door, waiting for the
Buddha to reach out his hand, take a banana, peel it,
and eat it. He waited and waited, but nothing happened. The Buddha did not seem to eat bananas,
unless he realized that someone was spying on him.

Thich Thanh Van told me several other stories
about when he was a young boy. When he discovered that the statue of the Buddha is not the Buddha,
he began to ask where the Buddhas are, because it
did not seem to him that Buddhas were living among
humans. He concluded that Buddhas must not be
very nice, because when people became Buddhas,
they would leave us to go to a faraway country. I told
him that Buddhas are us. They are made of flesh and
bones, not copper or silver or gold. The Buddha
statue is just a symbol of the Buddha, in the same
way the American flag is a symbol of America. The
American flag is not the American people.

The root-word *budh* means to wake up, to know, to
understand; and he or she who wakes up and understands is called a Buddha. It is as simple as that. The
capacity to wake up, to understand, and to love is
called Buddha nature. When Buddhists say, "I take
refuge in the Buddha," they are expressing trust in
their own capacity of understanding, of becoming
awake. The Chinese and the Vietnamese say, "I go
back and rely on the Buddha in me." Adding "in me"
makes it very clear that you yourself are the Buddha.

In Buddhism, there are three gems: Buddha, the awakened one; Dharma, the way of understanding and loving; and Sangha, the community that lives in harmony and awareness. The three are interrelated, and at times it is hard to distinguish one from another. In everyone there is the capacity to wake up, to understand, and to love. So in ourselves we find Buddha, and we also find Dharma and Sangha. I will explain more about Dharma and Sangha, but first I want to say something about Buddha, the one who develops his or her understanding and loving to the highest degree. (In Sanskrit, understanding is *prajña* and love is *karuna* and *maitri*.)

Understanding and love are not two things, but just one. Suppose your son wakes up one morning and sees that it is already quite late. He decides to wake up his younger sister, to give her enough time to eat breakfast before going to school. It happens that she is grouchy and instead of saying, "Thank you for waking me up," she says, "Shut up! Leave me alone!" and kicks him. He will probably get angry, thinking, "I woke her up nicely. Why did she kick me?" He may want to go to the kitchen and tell you about it, or even kick her back. But then he remembers that during the night his sister coughed a lot, and he realizes that she must be sick. Maybe she has a cold, maybe that is why she behaved so meanly. He is not angry anymore. At that moment there is *budh* in him. He understands, he is awake. When you understand, you cannot help but love. You cannot get angry. To develop understanding, you have to practice looking at all living beings with the eyes of compassion. When you understand, you love. And when you love, you naturally act in a way that can relieve the suffering of people.

Someone who is awake, who knows, who understands, is called a Buddha. Buddha is in everyone of us. We can become awake, understanding, and also loving. I often tell children that if their mother or father is very understanding and loving, working, taking care of the family, smiling, being lovely, like a flower, they can say, "Mommy (or Daddy), you are all Buddha today."

*   *   *

Two thousand five hundred years ago there was a person who practiced in a way that his understanding and love became perfected, and everyone in the world recognized this. His name was Siddhartha. When Siddhartha was very young, he began to think that life had a lot of suffering in it, that people do not love each other enough, do not understand each other enough. So he left his home to go to the forest to practice meditating, breathing, and smiling. He became a monk, and he tried to practice in order to develop his awakening, his understanding, and his love to the highest levels. He practiced sitting meditation and walking meditation for several years with five friends who were also monks. Although they were intelligent people, they made mistakes. For instance, each day they ate only one piece of fruit—one mango, or one guava, or one star fruit. Sometimes people exaggerate, and say that Siddhartha ate only one sesame seed a day, but I went to the forest in India where he practiced, and I know that is silly because there are no sesame seeds there. I saw also the Neranjara River, in which he bathed several times, and the Bodhi tree where he sat and became a Buddha. The Bodhi tree I saw is not the same tree, it is the great-great-great-grand-child of the first Bodhi tree.

One day Siddhartha became so weak that he could not practice, and as he was an intelligent young man, he decided to go to the village and get something to eat—bananas or cake or anything. But as soon as he took four or five steps, he stumbled and fainted; he lost consciousness because he was too hungry. He would have died, but the village chief's daughter, Sujata, who was taking food to the forest gods, saw him and came over. She found that he was still alive, still breathing, but very weak, and so she took a bowl and poured some milk into his mouth. At first Siddhartha did not react, but then his lips moved and he began to drink the milk. He drank a whole bowl of milk, and he felt much better and slowly sat up. He looked beautiful, because Siddhartha was a very, very handsome person. Nowadays people make statues of him which are not very handsome. Sometimes they are even grouchy, without any smile on his face. But he was a very beautiful person, and Sujata thought that he must be the god of the mountain. She kneeled down and was

about to worship, but he stretched out his arm to tell
her not to, and he told her something. What do you
think he must have said to her?

He said, "Please give me another bowl of milk." He
saw that the milk was doing wonderful things, and he
knew that once our body is strong enough, we can succeed in meditation. The young lady was so happy, she
poured him another bowl of milk. After that, she
inquired about him, and he said that he was a monk,
trying to meditate to develop his compassion and his
understanding to the highest level so that he could
help other people. She asked if there was anything she
could do to help, and Siddhartha said, "Each day at
noontime, can you give me a small bowl of rice? That
would help me very much." So from that day on, she
brought him some rice wrapped in banana leaves, and
sometimes she also brought milk.

The five other monks Siddhartha had been practicing with despised him and thought him worthless.
"Let us go somewhere else to practice. He drinks milk,
and he eats rice. He has no perseverance." But
Siddhartha did very well. Day in and day out he meditated, and he developed his insight, his understanding,
and his compassion very, very quickly as he recovered
his health.

One day, after taking a swim in the Neranjara River,
he had the impression that he only needed one more
sitting to come to a total breakthrough, to become a
fully enlightened person. When he was about to sit
down, still practicing walking meditation, a buffalo
boy came by. In India 2,500 years ago, buffaloes were

used to pull the plows, and a buffalo boy's job was
to watch them, bathe and take care of them, and cut
grass for them to eat.

As the buffalo boy came by, he saw Siddhartha
walking very peacefully, and he liked him immediately. Sometimes we see someone we like very much,
even if we don't know why. The boy wanted to say
something, but he was shy, so he came near
Siddhartha three or four times before saying,
"Gentleman, I like you very much." Siddhartha
looked at him and said, "I like you also."
Encouraged by this response, the boy told him, "I
really want to give you something, but I have nothing I can give you." And Siddhartha said, "You do
have something that I need. You have very beautiful
green grass that you just cut. If you want to, please
give me an armful of that grass." The boy was so
happy to be able to give him something, and
Siddhartha thanked him very much. After the buffalo boy left, Siddhartha spread the grass into a kind
of cushion that he could sit on.

As he sat down, he made a firm vow, "Until I get
true enlightenment, I shall not stand up." With this
strong determination, he meditated all night, and
when the morning star appeared in the sky, he
became a fully enlightened person, a Buddha, with
the highest capacity to understand and to love.

*   *   *

The Buddha stayed at that spot for two weeks, smiling and enjoying his breathing. Every day Sujata

brought him rice and the buffalo boy also came by to see him. He taught them about understanding, loving, and being awake. There is a scripture in the Pali Canon called *Sutta of Tending Buffaloes*, which lists eleven skills a buffalo boy must have, such as recognizing his own buffaloes, making smoke to keep mosquitoes away, taking care of wounds on the body of buffaloes, helping buffaloes cross rivers, and finding places with enough grass and water to eat. After listing eleven skills, the Buddha tells the monks that meditation is also like this, and he lists eleven parallel skills for monks—recognizing the five components of a human being, and so on. Most stories of the life of the Buddha overlook the two weeks he stayed near the Bodhi tree, meeting with Sujata and the buffalo boy, walking slowly, enjoying themselves. But I am sure it happened this way. Otherwise how could the Buddha have delivered the *Sutta of Tending Buffaloes*? In fact, when the buffalo boy grew up, he must have become a disciple of the Buddha, and one day, as he sat in the front of the assembly, the Buddha delivered that sutta.

*   *   *

After two weeks, the Buddha realized he had to get up from his seat under the Bodhi tree and share his understanding and compassion with other people. He told Sujata and the buffalo boy, "I am sorry, but I have to leave now. We are so happy together, but I must go and work with the adults."

He thought about who he could share his understanding and compassion with, and he thought of
the five friends who had practiced with him. He
walked an entire day in order to find them, and
when he happened upon their camp, they had just
finished their afternoon sitting meditation. They sat
a lot. They were very thin by now, as you can imagine. One of them saw the Buddha coming and said
to the others, "Don't stand up if he comes. Don't go
to the gate to welcome him. Don't go and fetch
water for him to wash his feet and his hands. He
didn't persevere. He ate rice, and he drank milk."
But when he arrived he was so attractive and so
peaceful that they could not help themselves from
offering him water to wash his feet and his hands
and giving him a special seat. The Buddha told
them, "Friends, I have found a way to develop
understanding and loving. Please sit down, I'll teach
you." They did not believe, at first. They said,
"Siddhartha, while we practiced together, you gave
up. You drank milk, you ate rice. How is it possible
you have become a fully enlightened person? Please
tell us. We cannot believe it." The Buddha said,
"Friends, have I ever told you a lie?" In fact, he had
never lied to anyone, and these five friends remem-
bered that. "I have never told you a lie. Now I am
not telling you a lie. I have become a fully enlightened person, and I'll be your teacher. Sit down, and
listen to me." And the five of them sat down and lis-
tened to the Buddha. He gave his first Dharma talk
for adults. If you want to read his words, they are

available in a wonderful sutta explaining the basic
doctrines of Buddhism: suffering, the causes of suffering, the removal of suffering, and the way to do it.

I have read many accounts of the life of the
Buddha, and I see him as a person like us. Sometimes
artists draw a Buddha in a way that we cannot recognize him as a human being. In fact, he is a human
being. I have seen so many Buddha statues, but not
many really beautiful and simple ones. If anytime you
want to draw a picture of a Buddha, please sit down
and breathe for five or ten minutes, smiling, before
you pick up the pen to draw a Buddha. Then draw a
simple Buddha, beautiful but simple, with a smile.
And if you can, draw some children sitting with him.
Buddha is young, not too grim, not too solemn, with a
very light smile on his face. We have to go in this
direction, because, when we look at the Buddha, we
have to like him just as the buffalo boy and Sujata
did.

*   *   *

When we say, "I take refuge in the Buddha," we
should also understand that "The Buddha takes
refuge in me," because without the second part the
first part is not complete. The Buddha needs us for
awakening, understanding, and love to be real things
and not just concepts. They must be real things that
have real effects on life. Whenever I say, "I take refuge
in the Buddha," I hear "Buddha takes refuge in me."
There is a verse for planting trees and other plants:

I entrust myself to earth,
Earth entrusts herself to me.
I entrust myself to Buddha,
Buddha entrusts herself to me.

"I entrust myself to earth" is like "I take refuge in the Buddha." (I identify myself with the plant.) The plant will die or be alive because of the earth. The plant takes refuge in the earth, the soil. But earth entrusts herself to me because each leaf that falls down and decomposes makes the soil richer. We know that the layer of soil that is rich and beautiful has been made by the vegetation. If our earth is green and beautiful, it is because of this vegetation. Therefore, while the vegetation needs the earth, the earth also needs the vegetation to express herself as a beautiful planet. So when we say, "I entrust myself to earth," I, the plant, have to hear the other version also: "Earth entrusts herself to me." "I entrust myself to Buddha, Buddha entrusts herself to me." Then it is very clear that the wisdom, the understanding and love of Shakyamuni Buddha needs us to be real again in life. Therefore, we have a very important task: to realize awakening, to realize compassion, to realize understanding.

We are all Buddhas, because only through us can understanding and love become tangible and effective. Thich Thanh Van was killed during his effort to help other people. He was a good Buddhist, he was a good Buddha, because he was able to help tens of thousands of people, victims of the war. Because

of him, awakening, understanding, and love were
real things. So we can call him a Buddha body, in
Sanskrit *Buddhakaya*. For Buddhism to be real, there
must be a Buddhakaya, an embodiment of awakened
activity. Otherwise Buddhism is just a word. Thich
Thanh Van was a Buddhakaya. Shakyamuni was a
Buddhakaya. When we realize awakening, when we
are understanding and loving, each of us is a
Buddhakaya.

*   *   *

The second gem is the Dharma. Dharma is what the
Buddha taught. It is the way of understanding and
love—how to understand, how to love, how to make
understanding and love into real things. Before the
Buddha passed away, he said to his students, "Dear
people, my physical body will not be here tomorrow,
but my teaching body will always be here to help.
You can consider it as your own teacher, a teacher
who never leaves you." That is the birth of
Dharmakaya. The Dharma has a body also, the body
of the teaching, or the body of the way. As you can
see, the meaning of Dharmakaya is quite simple,
although people in Mahayana have made it very
complicated. Dharmakaya just means the teaching of
the Buddha, the way to realize understanding and
love. Later it became something like the ontological
ground of being.

Anything that can help you wake up has Buddha
nature. When I am alone and a bird calls me, I return
to myself, I breathe, and I smile, and sometimes it

calls me once more. I smile and I say to the bird, "I hear already." Not only sounds, but sights can remind you to return to your true self. In the morning when you open your window and see the light streaming in, you can recognize it as the voice of the Dharma, and it becomes part of the Dharmakaya. That is why people who are awake see the manifestation of the Dharma in everything. A pebble, a bamboo tree, the cry of a baby, anything can be the voice of the Dharma calling. We should be able to practice like that.

One day a monk came to Tue Trung, the most illustrious teacher of Buddhism in Vietnam in the thirteenth century, a time when Buddhism was flourishing in Vietnam. The monk asked him, "What is the pure, immaculate Dharmakaya?", and Tue Trung pointed to the excrement of a horse. This was an irreverent approach to Dharmakaya, because people were using the word immaculate to describe it. You cannot use words to describe the Dharmakaya. Even though we say that it is immaculate, pure, that does not mean it is separate from things that are impure. Reality, ultimate reality, is free from all adjectives, either pure or impure. So his response was to shake up the mind of the monk, for him to cleanse himself of all these adjectives in order to see into the nature of the Dharmakaya. A teacher is also part of the Dharmakaya because she or he helps us be awake. The way she looks, the way she lives her daily life, the way she deals with people, animals, and plants helps us realize understanding and love in our life.

There are many ways of teaching: teaching by
words, teaching by books, teaching by tape recorders.
I have a friend who is a Zen teacher in Vietnam, quite
well known, but not many people can come and
study with him. Therefore, they make tape recordings
of his talks, and he has become known as Cassette
Monk! He is still in Vietnam. The government just
chased him away from his monastery, so he had to go
to another place to teach. He is not allowed to preach
in Ho Chi Minh City, because if he teaches there, too
many people come to hear him, and the government
doesn't like that.

Even if he does not teach, his being is very helpful
to us in being awake, for he is part of the
Dharmakaya. Dharmakaya is not just expressed in
words, in sounds. It can express itself in just being.
Sometimes if we don't do anything, we help more
than if we do a lot. We call that nonaction. It is like
the calm person on a small boat in a storm. That person does not have to do much, just to be himself and
the situation can change. That is also an aspect of
Dharmakaya: not talking, not teaching, just being.

This is true not only of humans, but other species
as well. Look at the trees in our yard. An oak tree is
an oak tree. That is all it has to do. If an oak tree is
less than an oak tree, then we are all in trouble.
Therefore, the oak tree is preaching the Dharma.
Without doing anything, not serving in the School
of Youth for Social Service, not preaching, not even
sitting in meditation, the oak tree is very helpful to
all of us just by being there. Every time we look at

the oak tree we have confidence. During the summer we sit under it and we feel cool, relaxed. We know that if the oak tree is not there, and all the other trees are not there, we will not have good air to breathe. We also know that in our former lives we were trees. Maybe we have been an oak tree ourselves. This is not just Buddhist; this is scientific. The human species is a very young species—we appeared on the earth only recently. Before that, we were rock, we were gas, we were minerals, and then we were single-celled beings. We were plants, we were trees, and now we have become humans. We have to recall our past existences. This is not difficult. You just sit down and breathe and look, and you can see your past existences. When we shout at the oak tree, the oak tree is not offended. When we praise the oak tree, it doesn't raise its nose. We can learn the Dharma from the oak tree; therefore, the oak tree is part of our Dharmakaya. We can learn from everything that is around, that is in us. Even if we are not at a meditation center, we can still practice at home, because around us the Dharma is present. Everything is preaching the Dharma. Each pebble, each leaf, each flower is preaching the *Saddharma Pundarika Sutra*.

*   *   *

The Sangha is the community that lives in harmony and awareness. *Sanghakaya* is a new Sanskrit term. The Sangha needs a body also. When you are with your family and you practice smiling, breathing, recognizing the Buddha body in yourself and your children, then your family becomes a Sangha. If you have a bell in your home, the bell becomes part of your Sanghakaya, because the bell helps you to practice. If you have a cushion, then the cushion also becomes part of the Sanghakaya. Many things help us practice. The air, for breathing. If you have a park or a riverbank near your home, you are very fortunate because you can enjoy practicing walking meditation. You have to discover your Sanghakaya, inviting a friend to come and practice with you, have tea meditation, sit with you, join you for walking meditation. All those efforts are to establish your Sanghakaya at home. Practice is easier if you have a Sanghakaya.

Siddhartha, the Buddha-to-be, while practicing with other people, began to drink milk, and the five monks who were with him went away. So he made the Bodhi tree into his Sanghakaya. He made the buffalo boy, the milkmaid, the river, the trees, and the birds around him into his Sanghakaya. There are those in Vietnam who live in reeducation camps. They don't have a Sangha. They don't have a Zen center. But they practice. They have to look upon other things as part of their Sanghakaya. I know of people who practiced walking meditation in their prison cells. They told me this after they got out of the camp. So while we are lucky, while we are still capable of finding so many elements to set up our Sanghakaya, we should do so. A friend, our own children, our own brother or sister, our house, the trees in our backyard, all of them can be part of our Sanghakaya.

Practicing Buddhism, practicing meditation is for us to be serene and happy, understanding and loving. In that way we work for the peace and happiness of our family and our society. If we look closely, the Three Gems are actually one. In each of them, the other two are already there. In Buddha, there is Buddhahood, there is the Buddha body. In Buddha there is the Dharma body because without the Dharma body, he could not have become a Buddha. In the Buddha there is the Sangha body because he had breakfast with the Bodhi tree, with the other trees, and birds and environment. In a meditation center, we have a Sangha body, Sanghakaya, because the way of understanding and compassion is practiced there. Therefore the Dharma body is present, the way, the teaching is present. But the teaching cannot become real without the life and body of each of us. So the Buddhakaya is also present. If Buddha and Dharma are not present, it is not a Sangha. Without you, the Buddha is not real, it is just an idea.

Without you, the Dharma cannot be practiced. It has to be practiced by someone. Without each of you, the Sangha cannot be. That is why when we say, "I take refuge in the Buddha," we also hear, "The Buddha takes refuge in me." "I take refuge in the Dharma. The Dharma takes refuge in me. I take refuge in the Sangha. The Sangha takes refuge in me."

Feelings and Perceptions

*A*ccording to Buddhism, human beings are composed of five aggregates: form, which means
our body, including the five sense organs and the nervous system; feelings; perceptions; mental forma-
tions; and consciousness. I would like to explain
about feelings and perceptions.

Every day we have many feelings. Sometimes we
are happy, sometimes we are sorrowful, sometimes
angry, irritated, or afraid; and these feelings fill our
mind and heart. One feeling lasts for a while, and
then another comes, and another, as if there is a
stream of feelings for us to deal with. Practicing meditation is to be aware of each feeling.

The Abhidharma writings on Buddhist psychology
say that feelings are of three kinds: pleasant, unpleasant, and neutral. When we step on a thorn, we
have an unpleasant feeling. When someone says

something nice to us, "You are very smart," or "You are very beautiful," we have a pleasant feeling. And there are neutral feelings, such as when you sit there and don't feel either pleasant or unpleasant. But I have read the Abhidharma and have practiced Buddhism, and I find this analysis not correct. A so-called neutral feeling can become very pleasant. If you sit down, very beautifully, and practice breathing and smiling, you can be very happy. When you sit in this way, aware that you have a feeling of well-being, that you don't have a toothache, that your eyes are capable of seeing forms and colors, isn't it wonderful?

For some people, working is unpleasant, and they suffer when they have to work. For other people, if they are forbidden from working, it is unpleasant. I do many kinds of work, and if you forbid me from binding books, from gardening, from writing poetry, from practicing walking meditation, from teaching children, I will be very unhappy. To me, work is pleasant. Pleasant or unpleasant depends on our way of looking.

We call seeing a neutral feeling. Yet someone who has lost her sight would give anything to be able to see, and if suddenly she could, she would consider it a miraculous gift. We who have eyes capable of seeing many forms and colors are often unhappy. If we want to practice, we can go out and look at leaves, flowers, children, and clouds, and be happy.

Whether or not we are happy depends on our awareness. When you have a toothache, you think that not having a toothache will make you very happy. But when you don't have a toothache, often you are still not happy. If you practice awareness, you suddenly become very rich, very very happy. Practicing Buddhism is a clever way to enjoy life. Happiness is available. Please help yourself to it. All of us have the capacity of transforming neutral feelings into pleasant feelings, very pleasant feelings that can last a long time. This is what we practice during sitting and walking meditation. If you are happy, all of us will profit from it. Society will profit from it. All living beings will profit from it.

On the wooden board outside of the meditation hall in Zen monasteries, there is a four-line inscription. The last line is, "Don't waste your life." Our lives are made of days and hours, and each hour is precious. Have we wasted our hours and our days? Are we wasting our lives? These are important questions. Practicing Buddhism is to be alive in each moment. When we practice sitting or walking, we have the means to do it perfectly. During the rest of the day, we also practice. It is more difficult, but it is possible. The sitting and the walking must be extended to the non-walking, non-sitting moments of our day. That is the basic principle of meditation.

*   *   *

Perceiving includes our ideas or concepts about reality. When you look at a pencil, you perceive it, but the pencil itself may be different from the pencil

in your mind. If you look at me, the me in myself
may be different from the me you perceive. In order
to have a correct perception, we need to have a
direct encounter.

When you look at the night sky, you might see a
very beautiful star, and smile at it. But a scientist
may tell you that the star is no longer there, that it
was extinct ten million years ago. So our perception
is not correct. When we see a very beautiful sunset,
we are very happy, perceiving that the sun is there
with us. In fact it was already behind the mountain
eight minutes ago. It takes eight minutes for the sunshine to reach our planet. The hard fact is that we
never see the sun in the present, we only see the sun
of the past. Suppose while walking in the twilight,
you see a snake, and you scream, but when you
shine your flashlight on it, it turns out to be a rope.
This is an error of perception. During our daily lives
we have many misperceptions. If I don't understand
you, I may be angry at you, all the time. We are not
capable of understanding each other, and that is the
main source of human suffering.

A man was rowing his boat upstream on a very
misty morning. Suddenly, he saw another boat coming downstream, not trying to avoid him. It was
coming straight at him. He shouted, "Be careful! Be
careful!" but the boat came right into him, and his
boat was almost sunk. The man became very angry,
and began to shout at the other person, to give him
a piece of his mind. But when he looked closely, he
saw that there was no one in the other boat. It

turned out that the boat just got loose and went downstream. All his anger vanished, and he laughed and he laughed. If our perceptions are not correct, they may give us a lot of bad feelings. Buddhism teaches us how to look at things deeply in order to understand their own true nature, so that we will not be misled into suffering and bad feelings.

*   *   *

The Buddha taught that this is like this, because that is like that. You see? Because you smile, I am happy. This is like this, therefore that is like that. And that is like that because this is like this. This is called dependent co-arising.

Suppose you and I are friends. (In fact, I hope we are friends.) My well-being, my happiness depends very much on you, and your well-being, your happiness, depends upon me. I am responsible for you, and you are responsible for me. Anything I do wrong, you will suffer, and anything you do wrong, I have to suffer. Therefore, in order to take care of you, I have to take care of myself.

There is a story in the Pali Canon about a father and a daughter who performed in the circus. The father would place a very long bamboo stick on his forehead, and his daughter would climb to the top of the stick. When they did this, people gave them some money to buy rice and curry to eat. One day the father told the daughter, "My dear daughter, we have to take care of each other. You have to take

care of your father, and I have to take care of you, so
that we will be safe. Our performance is very dangerous." Because if she fell, both would not be able to
earn their living. If she fell, then broke her leg, they
wouldn't have anything to eat. "My daughter, we
have to take care of each other so we can continue to
earn our living."

The daughter was wise. She said, "Father, you
should say it this way: 'Each one of us has to take
care of himself or herself, so that we can continue to
earn our living.' Because during the performance,
you take care of yourself, you take care of yourself
only. You stay very stable, very alert. That will help
me. And if when I climb I take care of myself, I climb
very carefully, I do not let anything wrong happen to
me. That is the way you should say it, Father. You
take good care of yourself, and I take good care of
myself. In that way we can continue to earn our living." The Buddha agreed that the daughter was right.

So we are friends, and our happiness depends on
each other. According to that teaching I have to take
care of myself, and you take care of yourself. That
way we help each other. And that is the most correct
perception. If I only say, "Don't do this, you have to
do that," and I don't take care of myself, I can do
many wrong things, and that does not help. I have to
take care of myself, knowing that I am responsible for
your happiness, and if you do the same, everything
will be all right. This is the Buddha's teaching about
perception, based on the principle of dependent co-
arising. Buddhism is easy to learn!

The Buddha had a special way to help us understand the object of our perception. He said that in
order to understand, you have to be one with what
you want to understand. This is a way that is practice-
able. About fifteen years ago, I used to help a committee for orphans, victims of the war in Vietnam. From
Vietnam, they sent out applications, one sheet of
paper with a small picture of a child in the corner,
telling the name, the age, and the conditions of the
orphan. We were supposed to translate it from
Vietnamese into French, English, Dutch, or German, in
order to seek a sponsor, so that the child would have
food to eat and books for school, and be put into the
family of an aunt or an uncle or a grandparent. Then
the committee could send the money to the family
member to help take care of the child.

Each day I helped translate about thirty applications into French. The way I did it was to look at the
picture of the child. I did not read the application, I
just took time to look at the picture of the child.
Usually after only thirty or forty seconds, I became
one with the child. I don't know how or why, but it's
always like that. Then I would pick up the pen and
translate the words from the application onto another
sheet. Afterwards I realized that it was not I who had
translated the application; it was the child and I, who
had become one. Looking at his face or her face, I got
motivated and I became him and he became me, and
together we did the translation. It is very natural. You
don't have to practice a lot of meditation to be able to
do that. You just look, you allow yourself to be, and

then you lose yourself in the child, and the child in you. This is one example which illustrates the way of perception recommended by Buddha. In order to understand something, you have to be one with that something.

The French language has the word *comprendre*, which means to understand, to know, to comprehend. *Com* means to be one, to be together, and *prendre* means to take or to grasp. To understand something is to take that thing up and to be one with it. The Indians have a wonderful example. If a grain of salt would like to measure the degree of saltiness of the ocean, to have a perception of the saltiness of the ocean, it drops itself into the ocean and becomes one with it, and the perception is perfect.

Nowadays, nuclear physicists have begun to feel the same way. When they get deeply into the world of subatomic particles, they see their mind in it. An electron is first of all your concept of the electron. The object of your study is no longer separated from your mind. Your mind is very much in it. Modern physicists think that the word *observer* is no longer valid, because an observer is distinct from the object he observes. They have discovered that if you retain that kind of distinction, you cannot go very far in subatomic nuclear science. So they have proposed the word *participant*. You are not an observer, you are a participant. That is the way I always feel when I give a lecture. I don't want the audience to be outside, to observe, to listen only. I want them to be one with me, to practice, to breathe. The speaker and the people who listen must become one in order for right perception to take place. Non-duality means "not two," but "not two" also means "not one." That is why we say "non-dual" instead of "one." Because if there is one, there are two. If you want to avoid two, you have to avoid one also.

In the *Satipatthana Sutta*, the basic manual on meditation from the time of the Buddha, it is recorded, "The practitioner will have to contemplate body in the body, feelings in the feelings, mind in the mind, objects of mind in the objects of mind." The words are clear. The repetition, "body in the body," is not just to underline the importance of it. Contemplating body in the body means that you do not stand outside of something to contemplate it. You must be one with it, with no distinction between the contemplator and the contemplated. Contemplating body in the body means that you should not look on your body as the object of your contemplation. You have to be one with it. The message is clear. Non-duality is the key word for Buddhist meditation.

*   *   *

To sit is not enough. We have to *be* at the same time. To be what? To be is to be a something, you cannot be a nothing. To eat, you have to eat something, you cannot just eat nothing. To be aware is to be aware of something. To be angry is to be angry at something. So to be is to be something, and that something is *what is going on*: in your body, in your mind, in your feelings, and in the world.

While sitting, you sit and you are. You are what? You are the breathing. Not only the one who breathes— you *are* the breathing and the smiling. It is like a television set of one million channels. When you turn the breathing on, you *are* the breathing. When you turn the irritation on, you are the irritation. You are one with it. Irritation and breathing are not things outside of you. You contemplate them in them, because you are one with them.

If I have a feeling of anger, how would I meditate on that? How would I deal with it, as a Buddhist, or as an intelligent person? I would not look upon anger as something foreign to me that I have to fight, to have surgery in order to remove it. I know that anger is me, and I am anger. Non-duality, not two. I have to deal with my anger with care, with love, with tenderness, with nonviolence. Because anger is me, I have to tend my anger as I would tend a younger brother or sister, with love, with care, because I myself am anger, I am in it, I am it. In Buddhism we do not consider anger, hatred, greed as enemies we have to fight, to destroy, to annihilate. If we annihilate anger, we annihilate our- selves. Dealing with anger in that way would be like transforming yourself into a battlefield, tearing yourself into parts, one part taking the side of Buddha, and one part taking the side of Mara. If you struggle in that way, you do violence to yourself. If you cannot be com- passionate to yourself, you will not be able to be com- passionate to others. When we get angry, we have to produce awareness: "I am angry. Anger is in me. I am anger." That is the first thing to do.

In the case of a minor irritation, the recognition of the presence of the irritation, along with a smile and a few breaths will usually be enough to transform the irritation into something more positive, like forgiveness, understanding, and love. Irritation is a destructive energy. We cannot destroy the energy; we can only convert it into a more constructive energy. Forgiveness is a constructive energy. Understanding is a constructive energy. Suppose you are in the desert, and you only have one glass of muddy water. You have to transform the muddy water into clear water to drink, you cannot just throw it away. So you let it settle for a while, and clear water will appear. In the same way, we have to convert anger into some kind of energy that is more constructive, because anger is you. Without anger you have nothing left. That is the work of meditation.

Earlier I gave the example of a big brother who got angry at his sister at first and then found out that she has a fever, and he understood and became concerned, and he tried to help her. So the destructive energy of anger, because of understanding, is transformed into the energy of love. Meditation on your anger is first of all to produce awareness of anger, "I am the anger," and then to look deeply into the nature of anger. Anger is born from ignorance, and is a strong ally of ignorance.

*   *   *

Perceptions are perceptions of our body, feelings, mind, nature, and society. We should have a good perception of the oak tree in order to see its Buddha nature, its function as a Dharma teacher. We have to perceive our political and economic systems correctly in order to see what is going wrong. Perception is very important for our well-being, for our peace. Perception should be free from emotions and ignorance, free from illusions.

In Buddhism, knowledge is regarded as an obstacle to understanding, like a block of ice that obstructs water from flowing. It is said that if we take one thing to be the truth and cling to it, even if truth itself comes in person and knocks at our door, we won't open it. For things to reveal themselves to us, we need to be ready to abandon our views about them.

The Buddha told a story about this. A young widower, who loved his five-year-old son very much, was away on business, and bandits came, burned down his whole village, and took his son away. When the man returned, he saw the ruins, and panicked. He took the charred corpse of an infant to be his own child, and he began to pull his hair and beat his chest, crying uncontrollably. He organized a cremation ceremony, collected the ashes and put them in a very beautiful velvet bag. Working, sleeping, eating, he always carried the bag of ashes with him.

One day his real son escaped from the robbers and found his way home. He arrived at his father's new cottage at midnight, and knocked at the door. You can imagine at that time, the young father was still carrying the bag of ashes, and crying. He asked,

"Who is there?" And the child answered, "It's me, Papa. Open the door, it's your son." In his agitated state of mind the father thought that some mischievous boy was making fun of him, and he shouted at the child to go away, and he continued to cry. The boy knocked again and again, but the father refused to let him in. Some time passed, and finally the child left. From that time on, father and son never saw one another. After telling this story, the Buddha said, "Sometime, somewhere you take something to be the truth. If you cling to it so much, when the truth comes in person and knocks at your door, you will not open it."

Guarding knowledge is not a good way to understand. Understanding means to throw away your knowledge. You have to be able to transcend your knowledge the way people climb a ladder. If you are on the fifth step of a ladder and think that you are very high, there is no hope for you to climb to the sixth. The technique is to release. The Buddhist way of understanding is always letting go of our views and knowledge in order to transcend. This is the most important teaching. That is why I use the image of water to talk about understanding. Knowledge is solid; it blocks the way of understanding. Water can flow, can penetrate.

The Heart of Practice

M editation is not to get out of society, to escape from society, but to prepare for a reentry into society. We call this "engaged Buddhism." When we go to a meditation center, we may have the impression that we leave everything behind—family, society, and all the complications involved in them— and come as an individual in order to practice and to search for peace. This is already an illusion, because in Buddhism there is no such thing as an individual.

Just as a piece of paper is the fruit, the combination of many elements that can be called non-paper elements, the individual is made of non-individual elements. If you are a poet, you will see clearly that there is a cloud floating in this sheet of paper. Without a cloud there will be no water; without water, the trees cannot grow; and without trees, you cannot make paper. So the cloud is in here. The existence of this page is dependent on the existence of a cloud. Paper and cloud are so close. Let us think of other things, like sunshine. Sunshine is very important because the forest cannot grow without sunshine, and we humans cannot grow without sunshine. So the logger needs sunshine in order to cut the tree, and the tree needs sunshine in order to be a tree. There-fore you can see sunshine in this sheet of paper. And if you look more deeply, with the eyes of a bodhisattva, with the eyes of those who are awake, you see not only the cloud and the sunshine in it, but that everything is here: the wheat that became the bread for the logger to eat, the logger's father— everything is in this sheet of paper.

The *Avatamsaka Sutra* tells us that you cannot point to one thing that does not have a relationship with this sheet of paper. So we say, "A sheet of paper is made of non-paper elements." A cloud is a non-paper element. The forest is a non-paper element. Sunshine is a non-paper element. The paper is made of all the non-paper elements to the extent that if we return the non-paper elements to their sources, the cloud to the sky, the sunshine to the sun, the logger to his father, the paper is empty. Empty of what? Empty of a separate self. It has been made by all the non-self elements, non-paper elements, and if all these non-paper elements are taken out, it is truly empty, empty of an independent self. Empty, in this sense, means that the paper is full of every-

thing, the entire cosmos. The presence of this tiny
sheet of paper proves the presence of the whole
cosmos.

In the same way, the individual is made of non-
individual elements. How do you expect to leave
everything behind when you enter a meditation
center? The kind of suffering that you carry in your
heart, that is society itself. You bring that with you,
you bring society with you. You bring all of us with
you. When you meditate, it is not just for yourself,
you do it for the whole society. You seek solutions
to your problems not only for yourself, but for all
of us.

Leaves are usually looked upon as the children of
the tree. Yes, they are children of the tree, born from
the tree, but they are also mothers of the tree. The
leaves combine raw sap, water, and minerals, with
sunshine and gas, and convert it into a variegated
sap that can nourish the tree. In this way, the leaves
become the mother of the tree. We are all children of
society, but we are also mothers. We have to nourish
society. If we are uprooted from society, we cannot
transform it into a more livable place for us and for
our children. The leaves are linked to the tree by a
stem. The stem is very important.

I have been gardening in our community for many
years, and I know that sometimes it is diffi-cult to
transplant cuttings. Some plants do not trans-plant
easily, so we use a kind of vegetable hormone to help
them be rooted in the soil more easily. I wonder
whether there is a kind of powder, something that

may be found in meditation practice that can help people who are uprooted be rooted again in society. Meditation is not an escape from society. Meditation is to equip oneself with the capacity to reintegrate into society, in order for the leaf to nourish the tree.

*   *   *

Something has happened in some meditation centers. A number of young people found themselves ill at ease with society, so they left in order to come to a meditation center. They ignored the reality that they did not come to the meditation center as an individual. Coming together in a meditation center, they form another kind of society. As a society, it has problems like other societies. Before entering the meditation center, they had hoped that they could find peace in meditation. Now, practicing and forming another kind of society, they discover that this society is even more difficult than the larger society. It is composed of alienated people. After some years, they feel frustrated, worse than before coming to the meditation center. This is because we misunderstand meditation, we misunderstand the purpose of meditation. Meditation is for everyone and not just for the person who meditates.

Bringing children into a meditation center is very natural. In Plum Village, children practice with adults. From time to time, we open the door for guests to come and practice with us, and bring their children. We especially take care of the children.

When the children are happy, the adults are happy. One day I overheard the children telling each other, "How come our parents are so nice here?" I have a friend who has been practicing meditation for fourteen years, and he has never shown his daughter how to meditate. You cannot meditate alone. You have to do it with your children. If your children are not happy, do not smile, you cannot smile. When you make a peaceful step, that is for you, but it is also for the children, and for the world.

I think that our society is a difficult place to live. If we are not careful, we can become uprooted, and once uprooted, we cannot help change society to make it more livable. Meditation is a way of helping us stay in society. This is very important. We have seen people who are alienated from society and cannot be reintegrated into society. We know that this can happen to us if we are not careful.

I have learned that many of the Buddhist practitioners in America are young and intellectual, and have come to Buddhism not by the door of faith, but by the door of psychology. I know people in the Western world suffer a great deal psychologically, and that is why many have become Buddhists, practicing meditation in order to solve psychological problems. Many are still in society, but some have been uprooted. Having lived for quite some time in this society, I myself feel that I cannot get along with this society very well. There are so many things that make me want to withdraw, to go back to myself. But my practice helps me remain in society, because

I am aware that if I leave society, I will not be able to help change it. I hope that those who are practicing Buddhism succeed in keeping their feet on earth, staying in society. That is our hope for peace.

*   *   *

I wrote a poem over thirty years ago, when I was twenty-seven or twenty-eight, about a brother who suffered so much he had to drop out of society and go to a meditation center. Since the Buddhist Temple is a place of compassion, they welcomed him. When someone is suffering so much, when he or she comes to a meditation center, the first thing is to give some kind of comfort. The people in the Temple were compassionate enough to let him come and have a place to cry. How long, how many days, how many years did he need to cry? We don't know. But finally he took up refuge in the meditation center and did not want to go back to society. He had had enough of it. He thought that he had found some peace, but one day I myself came and burned his meditation center, which was only a small hut: his last shelter! In his understanding, he had nothing else outside of that small cottage. He had nowhere to go because society was not his. He thought he had come to seek his own emancipation, but, in the light of Buddhism, there is no such thing as individual self. As we know, when you go into a Buddhist center, you bring with you all the scars, all the wounds from society, and you bring the whole society as well. In this poem, I am the

young man, and I am also the person who came and
burned down the cottage.

If you ask how much do I want,
I'll tell you that I want it all.
This morning, you and I
and all men
are flowing into the marvelous stream
of oneness.

Small pieces of imagination as we are,
we have come a long way to find ourselves
and for ourselves, in the dark, the illusion
of emancipation.

This morning, my brother is back from his
long adventure.
He kneels before the altar,
his eyes full of tears.
His soul is longing for a shore to set anchor at
(a yearning I once had).
Let him kneel there and weep.
Let him cry his heart out.
Let him have his refuge there for a thousand years,
enough to dry all his tears.

One night, I will come
and set fire to his shelter,
the small cottage on the hill.
My fire will destroy everything
and remove his only life raft after a shipwreck.

In the utmost anguish of his soul,
the shell will break.
The light of the burning hut will witness
his glorious deliverance.
I will wait for him
beside the burning cottage.
Tears will run down my cheeks.
I will be there to contemplate his new being.
And as I hold his hands in mine
and ask him how much he wants,
he will smile and say that he wants it all—
just as I did.

To me, a meditation center is where you get back to
yourself, you get a clearer understanding of reality,
you get more strength in understanding and love,
and you prepare for your reentry into society. If it is
not like that, it is not a real meditation center. As we
develop real understanding, we can reenter society
and make a real contribution.

*   *   *

We have many compartments in our lives. When we
practice sitting meditation and when we do not practice sitting, these two periods of time are so different
from each other. While sitting, we practice intensively
and while we are not sitting, we do not practice
intensively. In fact, we practice non-practice intensively. There is a wall which separates the two, prac-

ticing and non-practicing. Practicing is only for the practice period and non-practicing is only for the non-practicing period. How can we mix the two together? How can we bring meditation out of the meditation hall and into the kitchen, and the office? How can the sitting influence the non-sitting time? If a doctor gives you an injection, not only your arm but your whole body benefits from it. If you practice one hour of sitting a day, that hour should be all twenty-four hours, and not just for that hour. One smile, one breath should be for the benefit of the whole day, not just for that moment. We must practice in a way that removes the barrier between practice and non-practice.

When we walk in the meditation hall, we make careful steps, very slowly. But when we go to the airport, we are quite another person. We walk very differently, less mindfully. How can we practice at the airport and in the market? That is engaged Buddhism. Engaged Buddhism does not only mean to use Buddhism to solve social and political problems, protesting against the bombs, and protesting against social injustice. First of all we have to bring Buddhism into our daily lives. I have a friend who breathes between telephone calls, and it helps her very much. Another friend does walking meditation between business appointments, walking mindfully between buildings in downtown Denver. Passersby smile at him, and his meetings, even with difficult persons, often turn out to be very pleasant, and very successful.

We should be able to bring the practice from the meditation hall into our daily lives. How can we practice to penetrate our feelings, our perceptions during daily life? We don't deal with our perceptions and our feelings only during sitting practice. We have to deal with them all the time. We need to discuss among ourselves how to do it. Do you practice breathing between phone calls? Do you practice smiling while cutting carrots? Do you practice relaxation after hours of hard work? These questions are very practical. If you know how to apply Buddhism to dinner time, leisure time, sleeping time, I think Buddhism will become engaged in your daily life. Then it will have a tremendous effect on social concerns. Buddha, Dharma, and Sangha become the matters of everyday life, each minute, each hour of our daily life, and not just a description of something far away.

*   *   *

Our mind is like a river, with many thoughts and feelings flowing along. From time to time, it is helpful to recite a *gatha*, a short verse, to remind us what is going on. When we focus our mind on a gatha, the gatha is our mind at that moment. The gatha fills our mind for half a second, or ten seconds, or one minute, and then we may have another gatha a little further downstream. While eating a silent meal, I recite a gatha to myself, and then I eat something. When the plate is empty, I recite another gatha, and drink a cup of tea. Suppose there is one hour of sitting in meditation, and then five hours of non-sitting, followed by three more hours of sitting, intensive practice. What is the relationship between the practice time and the non-practice time, the practice mind and the non-practice mind? Sitting is like a gatha, a long silent gatha. (Maybe it's not so silent.) My main concern is the effect the gatha has on the non-gatha state of mind.

An automobile driver will need signs from time to time to show him the way. The sign and the road are one, because you don't see the sign only where it appears, you see it all along the way, until the next sign. There is no difference between the signs and the road. That is what we should do while practicing gathas and sitting. Gathas help us get back to ourselves, and as soon as the gatha ends, we continue along the stream. If we do not realize the unity of the gathas and the rest of our life, between the signs and the road, then we would have in ourselves what the French call *cloisons étanches*. It means absolute compartmentalization, with no communication whatsoever between the two compartments. Not permeable. Between the gatha and the non-gatha state of mind is an absolute distinction, like the sitting and the non-sitting.

How can the gathas affect the non-gatha moments? How will the sitting permeate the non sitting hours? We must learn to practice so that one gatha, one minute of sitting will influence the rest of the day, one step made in walking meditation will have an effect on the rest of the day. Every action, every thought has an effect. Even if I just clap my hands, the effect is everywhere, even in faraway galaxies. Every sitting, every walking, every smile will have an effect on your own daily life, and the life of other people also, and practice must be based on that.

*   *   *

When we practice sitting and walking, we must pay attention to the quality of the sitting and the walking, not the quantity. We have to practice intelligently. We need to create the kind of practice that will fit our circumstance.

There is a story I would like to tell you about a woman who practices the invocation of the Buddha Amitabha's name. She is very tough, and she practices the invocation three times daily, using a wooden drum and a bell, reciting "Namo Amitabha Buddha" for one hour each time. When she arrives at one thousand times, she invites the bell to sound. (In Vietnamese, we don't say "strike" or "hit" a bell.) Although she has been doing this for ten years, her personality has not changed. She is still quite mean, shouting at people all the time.

A friend wanted to teach her a lesson, so one afternoon when she had just lit the incense, invited the bell to sound three times, and was beginning to recite "Namo Amitabha Buddha," he came to her door, and said, "Mrs. Nguyen, Mrs. Nguyen!" She found it very annoying because this was her time of practice, but he just stood at the front gate shouting her name. She said to herself, "I have to struggle against my anger, so I will ignore that," and she went on, "Namo Amitabha Buddha, Namo Amitabha Buddha."

The gentleman continued to shout her name, and her anger became more and more oppressive. She struggled against it, wondering, "Should I stop my recitation and go and give him a piece of my mind?" But she continued chanting, and she struggled very hard. Fire mounted in her, but she still tried to chant "Namo Amitabha Buddha." The gentleman knew it, and he continued to shout, "Mrs. Nguyen! Mrs. Nguyen!"

She could not bear it any longer. She threw away the bell and the drum. She slammed the door, went out to the gate and said, "Why, why do you behave like that? Why do you call my name hundreds of times like that?" The gentleman smiled at her and said, "I just called your name for ten minutes, and you are so angry. You have been calling the Buddha's name for ten years. Think how angry he must be by now!"

The problem is not to do a lot, but to do it correctly. If you do it correctly, you become kinder, nicer, more understanding and loving. When we practice sitting or walking we should pay attention to the quality and not the quantity. If we practice only for the quantity, then we are not very different from Mrs. Nguyen. I think she learned her lesson. I think she did better after that.

Working for Peace

*I*n Plum Village in France, we receive many letters from the refugee camps in Singapore, Malaysia, Indonesia, Thailand, and the Philippines, hundreds each week. It is very painful to read them, but we have to do it, we have to be in contact. We try our best to help, but the suffering is enormous, and sometimes we are discouraged. It is said that half the boat people die in the ocean; only half arrive at the shores in Southeast Asia.

There are many young girls, boat people, who are raped by sea pirates. Even though the United Nations and many countries try to help the government of Thailand prevent that kind of piracy, sea pirates continue to inflict much suffering on the refugees. One day we received a letter telling us about a young girl on a small boat who was raped by a Thai pirate.

She was only twelve, and she jumped into the ocean and drowned herself.

When you first learn of something like that, you get angry at the pirate. You naturally take the side of the girl. As you look more deeply you will see it differently. If you take the side of the little girl, then it is easy. You only have to take a gun and shoot the pirate. But we cannot do that. In my meditation I saw that if I had been born in the village of the pirate and raised in the same conditions as he was, I am now the pirate. There is a great likelihood that I would become a pirate. I cannot condemn myself so easily. In my meditation, I saw that many babies are born along the Gulf of Siam, hundreds every day, and if we educators, social workers, politicians, and others do not do something about the situation, in twenty-five years a number of them will become sea pirates. That is certain. If you or I were born today in those fishing villages, we might become sea pirates in twenty-five years. If you take a gun and shoot the pirate, you shoot all of us, because all of us are to some extent responsible for this state of affairs.

After a long meditation, I wrote this poem. In it, there are three people: the twelve-year-old girl, the pirate, and me. Can we look at each other and recognize ourselves in each other? The title of the poem is "Please Call Me By My True Names," because I have so many names. When I hear one of these names, I have to say, "Yes."

Do not say that I'll depart tomorrow
because even today I still arrive.

Look deeply: I arrive in every second
to be a bud on a spring branch,
to be a tiny bird, with wings still fragile,
learning to sing in my new nest,
to be a caterpillar in the heart of flower,
to be a jewel hiding itself in a stone.

I still arrive, in order to laugh and to cry,
in order to fear and to hope,
the rhythm of my heart is the birth and
death of all that are alive.

I am the mayfly metamorphosing
on the surface of the river,
and I am the bird which, when spring comes,
arrives in time to eat the mayfly.

I am the frog swimming happily
in the clear water of a pond,
and I am also the grass-snake who,
approaching in silence,
feeds itself on the frog.

I am the child in Uganda, all skin and bones,
my legs as thin as bamboo sticks,
and I am the arms merchant,
selling deadly weapons to Uganda.

I am the twelve-year-old girl,
refugee on a small boat,
who throws herself into the ocean
after being raped by a sea pirate,
and I am the pirate, my heart not yet capable
of seeing and loving.

I am a member of the politburo,
with plenty of power in my hands,
and I am the man who has to pay his
"debt of blood" to my people,
dying slowly in a forced labor camp.

My joy is like spring, so warm
it makes flowers bloom in all walks of life.
My pain is like a river of tears, so full
it fills up the four oceans.

Please call me by my true names,
so I can hear all my cries and my laughs at once,
so I can see that my joy and pain are one.

Please call me by my true names,
so I can wake up,
and so the door of my heart can be left open,
the door of compassion.

*   *   *

There is a Zen story about a man riding a horse that is galloping very quickly. Another man, standing alongside the road, yells at him, "Where are you going?" and the man on the horse yells back, "I don't know. Ask the horse." I think that is our situation. We are riding many horses that we cannot control. The proliferation of armaments, for instance, is a horse. We have tried our best, but we cannot control these horses. Our lives are so busy.

In Buddhism, the most important precept of all is to live in awareness, to know what is going on. To know what is going on, not only here, but there. For instance, when you eat a piece of bread, you may choose to be aware that our farmers, in growing the wheat, use chemical poisons a little too much. Eating the bread, we are somehow co-responsible for the destruction of our ecology. When we eat a piece of meat or drink alcohol, we can produce awareness that 40,000 children die *each day* in the Third World from hunger and that in order to produce a piece of meat or a bottle of liquor, we have to use a lot of grain. Eating a bowl of cereal may be more reconciling with the suffering of the world than eating a piece of meat. An authority on economics who lives in France told me that if only the people in Western countries would reduce the eating of meat and the drinking of alcohol by 50 percent, that would be enough to change the situation of the world. Only 50 percent less.

Every day we do things, we are things, that have to do with peace. If we are aware of our lifestyle, our way of consuming, of looking at things, we will know how to make peace right in the moment we are alive, the present moment. When we pick up the Sunday newspaper, for instance, we may be aware that it is a very heavy edition, maybe three or four pounds. To print such a paper, a whole forest may be needed. When we pick up the paper, we should be aware. If we are very aware, we can do something to change the course of things.

*   *   *

In my temple, I was the first monk to ride a bicycle. At that time, there were no gathas to recite while riding on a bicycle. We have to practice intelligently, to keep the practice up to date, so recently I wrote a gatha you can use before you start your car. I hope you will find it helpful:

> Before starting the car,
> I know where I am going.
> The car and I are one.
> If the car goes fast, I go fast.

Sometimes we don't really need to use the car, but because we want to get away from ourselves, we go down and start the car. If we recite the gatha, "Before starting the car, I know where I am going," it can be like a flashlight—we may see that we don't need to go anywhere. Anywhere we go, we will have our self with us; we cannot escape ourselves. Sometimes it is better to turn the engine off and go

out for a walking meditation. It may be more pleasant to do that.

It is said that in the last few years, two million
square miles of forest land have been destroyed by
acid rain, and that is partly because of our cars.
"Before starting the car, I know where I am going," is
a very deep question. "Where shall I go? To my own
destruction?" If the trees die, humans are going to die
also. If trees and animals are not alive, how can we
be alive?

"The car and I are one." We have the impression
that we are the boss, and the car is only an instrument, but that is not true. With the car, we become
something different. With a gun, we become very
dangerous. With a flute, we become pleasant. With
50,000 atomic bombs, humankind has become the
most dangerous species on earth. We were never so
dangerous as we are now. We should be aware. The
most basic precept of all is to be aware of what we
do, what we are, each minute. Every other precept
will follow from that.

*   *   *

We have to look deeply at things in order to see.
When a swimmer enjoys the clear water of the river,
he or she should also be able to *be* the river. One day
I was having lunch at Boston University with some
friends, and I looked down at the Charles River. I
had been away from home for quite a long time, and
seeing the river, I found it very beautiful. So I left

my friends and went down to wash my face and dip
my feet in the water, as we used to do in our country.
When I returned, a professor said, "That's a very
dangerous thing to do. Did you rinse your mouth in
the river?" When I told him, "Yes," he said, "You
should see a doctor and get a shot."

I was shocked. I didn't know that the rivers here
are so polluted. You may call them dead rivers. In
our country the rivers get very muddy sometimes,
but not that kind of dirt. Someone told me that there
are so many chemicals in the Rhine River in Germany
that it is possible to develop photographs in it. We
can be good swimmers, but can we be a river and
experience the fears and hopes of a river? If we cannot, then we do not have the chance for peace. If all
the rivers are dead, then the joy of swimming in the
river will no longer exist.

If you are a mountain climber or someone who
enjoys the countryside, or the green forest, you know
that the forests are our lungs outside of our bodies.
Yet we have been acting in a way that has allowed
two million square miles of forest land to be destroyed by acid rain. We are imprisoned in our small
selves, thinking only of the comfortable conditions
for this small self, while we destroy our large self.
One day I suddenly saw that the sun is my heart, my
heart outside of this body. If my body's heart ceases
to function I cannot survive; but if the sun, my other
heart, ceases to function, I will also die immediately.
We should be able to be our true self. That means
we should be able to be the river, we should be able

to be the forest, we should be able to be a Soviet citizen. We must do this to understand, and to have hope for the future. That is the non-dualistic way of seeing.

*   *   *

During the war in Vietnam we young Buddhists organized ourselves to help victims of the war rebuild villages that had been destroyed by the bombs. Many of us died during service, not only because of the bombs and the bullets, but because of the people who suspected us of being on the other side. We were able to understand the suffering of both sides, the communists and the anti-communists. We tried to be open to both, to understand this side and to understand that side, to be one with them. That is why we did not take a side, even though the whole world took sides. We tried to tell people our perception of the situation: that we wanted to stop the fighting, but the bombs were so loud. Sometimes we had to burn ourselves alive to get the message across, but even then the world could not hear us. They thought we were supporting a kind of political act. They didn't know that it was a purely human action to be heard, to be understood. We wanted reconciliation, we did not want a victory. Working to help people in a circumstance like that is very dangerous, and many of us got killed. The communists killed us because they suspected that we were working with the Americans, and the anti-communists killed us be-

cause they thought that we were with the communists. But we did not want to give up and take one
side.

The situation of the world is still like this. People
completely identify with one side, one ideology. To
understand the suffering and the fear of a citizen of
the Soviet Union, we have to become one with him or
her. To do so is dangerous—we will be suspected by
both sides. But if we don't do it, if we align ourselves
with one side or the other, we will lose our chance to
work for peace. Reconciliation is to understand both
sides, to go to one side and describe the suffering
being endured by the other side, and then to go to the
other side and describe the suffering being endured
by the first side. Doing only that will be a great help
for peace.

During a retreat at the Providence Zen Center, I
asked someone to express himself as a swimmer in a
river, and then after fifteen minutes of breathing, to
express himself as the river. He had to become the
river to be able to express himself in the language and
feelings of the river. After that a woman who had
been in the Soviet Union was asked to express herself
as an American, and after some breathing and meditation, as a Soviet citizen, with all her fears and her
hope for peace. She did it wonderfully. These are exer-
cises of meditation related to non-duality.

The young Buddhist workers in Vietnam tried to
do this kind of meditation. Many of them died during
service. I wrote a poem for my young brothers and

sisters on how to die nonviolently, without hatred. It
is called "Recommendation":

> Promise me,
> promise me this day,
> promise me now,
> while the sun is overhead
> exactly at the zenith,
> promise me:
>
> Even as they
> strike you down
> with a mountain of hatred and violence;
> even as they step on you and crush you
> like a worm,
> even as they dismember and disembowel you,
> remember, brother,
> remember:
> man is not our enemy.
>
> The only thing worthy of you is compassion—
> invincible, limitless, unconditional.
> Hatred will never let you face
> the beast in man.
>
> One day, when you face this beast alone,
> with your courage intact, your eyes kind,
> untroubled
> (even as no one sees them),
> out of your smile
> will bloom a flower.

And those who love you
will behold you
across ten thousand worlds of birth and dying.

Alone again,
I will go on with bent head,
knowing that love has become eternal.
On the long, rough road,
the sun and the moon
will continue to shine.

To practice meditation is to be aware of the existence
of suffering. The first Dharma talk that the Buddha
gave was about suffering, and the way out of suffering. In South Africa, the black people suffer enor-
mously, but the white people also suffer. If we take
one side, we cannot fulfill our task of reconciliation in
order to bring about peace.

Are there people who can be in touch with both
the black community and the white community in
South Africa? If there are not many of them, the situation is bad. There must be people who can get in
touch with both sides, understanding the suffering of
each, and telling each side about the other. Are there
people doing that kind of understanding and mediation and reconciliation between the two major political blocs on the earth? Can you be more than
Americans? Can you be people who understand
deeply the suffering of both sides? Can you bring the
message of reconciliation?

*   *   *

You may not be aware that your country has been
manufacturing a lot of conventional weapons to sell
to Third World countries for their people to kill each
other. You know very well that children and adults in
these countries need food more than these deadly
weapons. Yet no one has the time to organize a
national debate to look at the problem of manufacturing and selling these deadly things. Everyone is too
busy. Conventional weapons have been killing in the
last thirty, forty, fifty years, very much. If we only
think of the nuclear bombs that may explode in the
future and do not pay attention to the bombs that are
exploding in the present moment, we commit some
kind of error. I believe President Reagan said that the
U.S. has to continue to make conventional weapons
to sell because if you don't, someone else will and the
U.S. will lose its interest. This is not a good thing to
say. It is off course. This statement is just an excuse,
but there are real factors that push him and push the
whole nation to continue to manufacture conventional weapons to sell. For instance, many people will
lose their jobs if they stop. Have we thought about
the kind of work that will help these people if the
weapons industry stops?

Not many Americans are aware that these
weapons are killing people in the Third World every
day. The Congress has not debated this issue seriously. We have not taken the time to see this situation
clearly, so we have not been able to change our government's policy. We are not strong enough to pres-

sure the government. The foreign policy of a government is largely dictated by its people and their way
of life. We have a large responsibility as citizens. We
think that the government is free to make policy, but
that freedom depends on our daily life. If we make it
possible for them to change policies, they will do it.
Now it is not yet possible. Maybe you think that if
you get into government and obtain power, you can
do anything you want, but that is not true. If you
become president, you will be confronted by this
hard fact. You will probably do just the same thing, a
little better or a little worse.

Therefore we have to see the real truth, the real situation. Our daily lives, the way we drink, what we
eat, has to do with the world's political situation.
Meditation is to see deeply into things, to see how we
can change, how we can transform our situation. To
transform our situation is also to transform our
minds. To transform our minds is also to transform
our situation, because the situation is mind, and
mind is situation. Awakening is important. The
nature of the bombs, the nature of injustice, the
nature of the weapons, and the nature of our own
beings are the same. This is the real meaning of
engaged Buddhism.

*   *   *

During the last 2,500 years in Buddhist monasteries, a
system of seven practices of reconciliation has
evolved. Although these techniques were formulated

to settle disputes within the circle of monks, I think
they might also be of use in our households and in
our society.

The first practice is **Face-to-Face Sitting**. In a con-
vocation of the whole sangha, everyone sits together
mindfully, breathing and smiling, with the willingness to help, and not with the willingness to fight.
This is basic. The two conflicting monks are present,
and they know that everyone in the community
expects them to make peace. Even before anything is
said, the atmosphere of peace is already present.
People refrain from listening to stories outside of the
assembly, spreading news about this monk or other
monks, commenting on the behavior of this monk or
the other monks. That would not help. Everything
must be said in public, in the community. So the two
monks are sitting facing each other, breathing and,
how hard, smiling.

The second practice is **Remembrance**. Both monks
try to remember the whole history of the conflict,
every detail having to do with the conflict, while the
whole assembly just sits patiently and listens: "I
remember that that day it was rainy, and I went to
the kitchen and you were there. . . ," telling as much
he can recall. This is quite important, because the
monks are trying to mend the things of the past. The
principle of sangha life is to be aware of what is
going on every day. If you are not aware of what is
going on, one day things will explode, and it will be
too late. If the community is sitting in assembly and
there are two monks confronting each other, already

the conflict has exploded into the open. To sit and try
to recall details from the past is the only thing to do
now, as far as the past is concerned.

Suppose a woman and a man get married and
then live a neglectful life, not knowing what is really
going on subconsciously. Their feelings and their
perceptions are creating a dangerous situation. Sometimes things occur beneath the surface that will even-
tually explode, and by then it is too late to deal with
them, so the only recourse is divorce or fighting or
even killing each other. To meditate is to be aware of
what is going on in yourself, your feelings, your
body, your perceptions, your family. This is very
important for any kind of life. The second technique
is to recall, and the more details which the community has, the easier it is to help.

The third principle is **Non-stubbornness**.
Everyone in the community expects the two monks
not to be stubborn, to try their best for reconciliation.
The outcome is not important. The fact that each
monk is doing his best to show his willingness for
reconciliation and understanding is most important.
When you do your best, trying to be your best in
understanding and accepting, you don't have to
worry about the outcome. You do your best, and that
is enough. The other person will do his or her best.
The atmosphere of the assembly is crucial. Because
everyone has high expectations for the two monks,
they know they must act well or they will not be recognized as brothers.

The fourth practice is **Covering Mud with Straw**. You know when you walk in the countryside after a rain, it is very muddy. If you have straw to spread over the mud, you can walk safely. One respected senior monk is appointed to represent each side of the conflict. These two monks then address the assembly, trying to say something to de-escalate the feeling in the concerned people. In a Buddhist sangha, people respect the high monks. We call them ancestral teachers. They don't have to say very much; whatever they say is taken very seriously by the rest of the community. One says something concerning this monk, and what he says will cause the other monk to understand better and de-escalate his feeling, his anger or his resistance. Then the other high monk says something to protect the other monk, saying it in a way that the first monk feels better. By doing so, they dissipate the hard feelings in the hearts of the two monks and help them to accept the verdict proposed by the community. Putting straw on mud— the mud is the dispute, and the straw is the lovingkindness of the Dharma.

The next stage is **Voluntary Confession**. Each monk reveals his own shortcomings, without waiting for others to say them. If the others say them, you feel differently. If you yourself say them, it is wonderful. First you reveal a minor weakness. You may have a big weakness, but you tell only of some minor transgression. (There is an art in all that.) As you make a confession, you might say, "On that day, I was not very mindful. I said such and such a thing. That is horrible. I am sorry." Even though it is a very minor confession, it helps the other person feel better. It encourages him to confess something of the same magnitude. (Imagine the Soviet Union and the United States trying to slowly de-escalate the small things.)

This atmosphere is encouraging. Everyone is supportive, expecting that de-escalation will be realized. The Buddha nature in each monk has the opportunity to come out, and the pressure on each monk from his anger or resentment will lighten. In this kind of atmosphere, the capacity of mutual understanding and acceptance will be born. Then the senior monks remind the feuding monks, "First of all you are part of the community. The well-being of the community is most important. Don't think only of your own feeling. Think of the well-being of the community." And then each monk will be ready to make a sacrifice, and get ready to accept the verdict or decision made by the community.

The sixth and seventh practices are **Decision by Consensus** and **Accepting the Verdict**. It is agreed in advance that the two monks will accept whatever verdict is pronounced by the whole assembly, or they will have to leave the community. So, after exploring every detail of the conflict, after realizing the maximum of reconciliation, a committee presents a verdict. It is announced three times. The head of the community reads the decision in this way: "After meditation, after exploration, after discussion, after all efforts have been made, it is suggested that this monk will do so and so, that monk will do so and so, this should be repaired in this way, that should be repaired in that way. Does the assembly of monks accept this verdict?" If the community remains silent, that means, "Okay." Then he repeats exactly the same words, "Does the noble assembly accept this verdict?" And then, silence. And a third time, "Does the community accept this verdict?" After a third time of silence, he pronounces, "The noble community of monks and nuns has accepted the verdict. Please, both sides carry out the decision." This is the end of the session. There may be many sessions to solve one case. If one of the monks rebels against the verdict, his voice is of no weight, because he has already agreed to obey any verdict made by the assembly.

These seven methods of settling disputes have been adopted by Buddhist monks and nuns in India, China, Vietnam, Japan, Korea, and many other countries for more than 2,500 years. I think we can learn something from them to apply in our own households and society.

*   *   *

In the peace movement there is a lot of anger, frustration, and misunderstanding. The peace movement can write very good protest letters, but they are not yet able to write a love letter. We need to learn to write a letter to the Congress or to the president of the United States that they will want to read, and not just throw away. The way you speak, the kind of understanding, the kind of language you use should not turn people off. The president is a person like any of us.

Can the peace movement talk in loving speech, showing the way for peace? I think that will depend on whether the people in the peace movement can be peace. Because without being peace, we cannot do anything for peace. If we cannot smile, we cannot help other people to smile. If we are not peaceful, then we cannot contribute to the peace movement.

I hope we can bring a new dimension to the peace movement. The peace movement is filled with anger and hatred. It cannot fulfill the path we expect from them. A fresh way of being peace, of doing peace is needed. That is why it is so important for us to practice meditation, to acquire the capacity to look, to see, and to understand. It would be wonderful if we could bring to the peace movement our contribution, our way of looking at things, that will diminish aggression and hatred. Peace work means, first of all, being peace. Meditation is meditation for all of us. We rely on each other. Our children are relying on us in order for them to have a future.

Interbeing

I believe that the encounter between Buddhism and the West will bring about something very exciting, very important. There are important values in Western society, such as the scientific way of looking at things, the spirit of free inquiry, and democracy. If there is an encounter between Buddhism and these values, humankind will have something very new, very exciting. Let us look at some examples: Printing was invented in China and movable metal type was invented in Korea, but when the West began printing, it became a very important means for communication. Gunpowder was discovered by the Chinese, but when it came to be manufactured by Westerners, it changed the face of the Earth. And the tea that was discovered in Asia, when brought to the West, has become tea bags. When combined with the Western way of doing things, the Buddhist principle of seeing and acting non-dualistically will totally change our way of life. The role of American Buddhists in bringing Buddhism into the encounter with Western civilization is very important for all of us.

Buddhism is not one. The teaching of Buddhism is many. When Buddhism enters one country, that country always acquires a new form of Buddhism. The first time I visited Buddhist communities in this country I asked a friend, "Please show me your Buddha, your American Buddha." The question surprised my friend, because he thought that the Buddha is universal. In fact, the Chinese have a Chinese Buddha, Tibetans have a Tibetan Buddha, and also the teaching is different. The teaching of Buddhism in this country is different from in other countries. Buddhism, in order to be Buddhism, must be suitable, appropriate to the psychology and the culture of the society that it serves.

My question was a very simple question. "Where is your Bodhisattva? Show me an American Bodhisattva." My friend was not capable of doing that. "Show me an American monk, an American nun, or an American Buddhist Center." All these things are not apparent yet. I think we can learn from other Buddhist traditions, but you have to create your own Buddhism. I believe that out of deep practice you will have your own Buddhism very soon.

*   *   *

I would like to present to you a form of Buddhism that may be accepted here in the West. In the past twenty years we have been experimenting with this form of Buddhism, and it seems that it may be suitable for our modern society. It is called the Tiep Hien Order, the Order of "Interbeing."

The Tiep Hien Order was founded in Vietnam during the war. It derives from the Zen School of Lin Chi, and is the forty-second generation of this school. It is a form of engaged Buddhism, Buddhism in daily life, in society, and not just in a retreat center. *Tiep* and *hien* are Vietnamese words of Chinese origin. I would like to explain the meaning of these words, because understanding them helps in understanding the spirit of this order.

Tiep means "to be in touch." The notion of engaged Buddhism already appears in the word tiep. First of all, to be in touch with oneself. In modern society most of us don't want to be in touch with ourselves; we want to be in touch with other things like religion, sports, politics, a book—we want to forget ourselves. Anytime we have leisure, we want to invite something else to enter us, opening ourselves to the television and telling the television to come and colonize us. So first of all, "in touch" means in touch with oneself in order to find out the source of wisdom, understanding, and compassion in each of us. Being in touch with oneself is the meaning of meditation, to be aware of what is going on in your body, in your feelings, in your mind. That is the first meaning of tiep.

Tiep also means to be in touch with Buddhas and bodhisattvas, the enlightened people in whom full understanding and compassion are tangible and effective. Being in touch with oneself means being in touch with this source of wisdom and compassion. You know that children understand that the Buddha is in themselves. One young boy claimed to be a Buddha on the first day of a retreat in Ojai, California. I told him that this is partly true, because sometimes he is Buddha, but sometimes he is not; it depends on his degree of being awake.

The second part of the meaning of tiep is "to continue," to make something more long-lasting. It means that the career of understanding and compassion started by Buddhas and bodhisattvas should be continued. This is possible only if we get in touch with our true self, which is like digging deep into the soil until we reach a hidden source of fresh water, and then the well is filled. When we are in touch with our true mind, the source of understanding and compassion will spring out. This is the basis of everything. Being in touch with our true mind is necessary for the continuation of the career started by the Buddhas and bodhisattvas.

Hien means "the present time." We have to be in the present time, because only the present is real, only in the present moment can we be alive. We do not practice for the sake of the future, to be reborn in a paradise, but to be peace, to be compassion, to be joy right now. Hien also means "to make real, to manifest, realization." Love and understanding are not only concepts and words. They must be real things, realized, in oneself and in society. That is the meaning of the word hien.

It is difficult to find English or French words which convey the same meaning as *Tiep Hien*. There is a term from the *Avatamsaka Sutra*, "interbeing," that conveys the spirit, so we have translated Tiep Hien as interbeing. In the sutra it is a compound term which means "mutual" and "to be." Interbeing is a new word in English, and I hope it will be accepted. We have talked about the many in the one, and the one containing the many. In one sheet of paper, we see everything else, the cloud, the forest, the logger. I am, therefore you are. You are, therefore I am. That is the meaning of the word "interbeing." We interare.

In the Order of Interbeing, there are two communities. The Core Community consists of lay and monastic men and women who have taken the vow to observe the Fourteen Mindfulness Trainings of the Order. Before being ordained as a brother or a sister of the Order of Interbeing, one should practice at least one year in this way. Upon ordination, the person has to organize a community around himself or herself in order to continue the practice. That community is called the Extended Community. This means all those who practice exactly the same way, but have not taken the vow, have not been ordained into the Core Community.

The lay people who are ordained into the Core Community do not have any special sign at all. They don't shave their heads, they do not have a special robe, except sometimes they wear a brown jacket. What makes them different is that they observe a number of rules, one of which is to practice at least sixty days of retreat, days of mindfulness, each year, whether consecutively or divided into several periods. If they practice every Sunday, for instance, they will have fifty-two already. The people in the Extended Community can do that, or more, even if they don't want to be ordained. In the Core Community people can choose to observe celibacy or lead a family life.

At least once every two weeks, members and friends come together and recite the Fourteen Mindfulness Trainings. They begin with the three refuges and the two promises for children. These two promises envelop all the mindfulness trainings of the adults. The first promise is: "I vow to develop my compassion in order to love and protect the life of people, animals, plants, and minerals." The second promise is: "I vow to develop understanding in order to be able to love and to live in harmony with people, animals, plants, and minerals." So the two promises are compassion, or love, and understanding. They are the essence of the Buddha's teaching. After the children recite the three refuges and these two promises, they can go outside and play; and the adults recite their Fourteen Mindfulness Trainings.

Until recently, I have used the term "precepts" instead of "mindfulness trainings." But many Western friends told me that the word "precepts" evokes in them a strong feeling of good and evil, that if they "break" a precept, they feel they have completely failed. Precepts are different from "commandments." They are the insights born from directly observing suffering and the causes of suffering. They are the most concrete expression of the practice of mindfulness. That is why it is appropriate and helpful to describe them as "mindfulness trainings."

Precepts usually begin with admonitions concerning the body, such as "not to kill." The Mindfulness Trainings of the Order of Interbeing are the opposite—

the ones concerning the mind come first. According to the teachings of the Buddha, the mind is the root of everything else. These then are the Mindfulness Trainings of the Order of Interbeing:

First: Aware of the suffering created by fanaticism and intolerance, we are determined not to be idolatrous about or bound to any doctrine, theory, or ideology, even Buddhist ones. Buddhist teachings are guiding means to help us learn to look deeply and to develop our understanding and compassion. They are not doctrines to fight, kill, or die for.

This mindfulness training is the roar of the lion. Its spirit is characteristic of Buddhism. It is often said that the Buddha's teaching is only a raft to help you cross the river, a finger pointing to the moon. Don't mistake the finger for the moon. The raft is not the shore. If we cling to the raft, if we cling to the finger, we miss everything. We cannot, in the name of the finger or the raft, kill each other. Human life is more precious than any ideology or doctrine.

The Order of Interbeing was born in Vietnam during the war, which was a conflict between two world ideologies. In the name of ideologies and doctrines, people kill and are killed. If you have a gun, you can shoot one, two, three, five people; but if you have an ideology and stick to it, thinking it is the absolute truth, you can kill millions. This mindfulness training includes the admonition not to kill in its deepest sense. Humankind suffers very much from attachment to views. "If you don't follow this teaching, I will cut off your head." In the name of the truth, we kill each other. The world is stuck in that situation. There are people who still think that Marxism is the highest product of the human mind, that nothing can compare with it. Others think it is crazy, and that we have to destroy those people. We are caught in this situation.

One of the most basic teachings of the Buddha is that life is precious. Peace can only be achieved when we are free from fanaticism. The more you practice this mindfulness training, the deeper you will go into reality and understand the teaching of the Buddha.

Second: Aware of the suffering created by attachment to views and wrong perceptions, we are determined to avoid being narrow-minded and bound to present views. We shall learn and practice nonattachment from views in order to be open to others' insights and experiences. We are aware that the knowledge we presently possess is not changeless, absolute truth. Truth is found in life, and we will observe life within and around us in every moment, ready to learn throughout our lives.

This mindfulness training arises from the first one. Remember the young father who refused to open the door to his own son, thinking the boy was already dead. The Buddha said, "If you cling to something as absolute truth and are caught in it, when truth comes in person and knocks on your door, you will refuse to let it in." A scientist with an open mind, who can question the present knowledge of science, will have more of a chance of discovering a higher truth. A Buddhist in her quest for higher understanding, also has to question her present views concerning reality. The technique of understanding is to overcome views and knowledge. The way of nonattachment from views is the basic teaching of Buddhism concerning understanding.

Third: Aware of the suffering brought about when we impose our views on others, we are committed not to force others, even our children, by any means whatsoever—such as authority, threat, money, propaganda, or indoctrination—to adopt our views. We will respect the right of others to be different and to choose what to believe and how to decide. We will, however, help others renounce fanaticism and narrowness through compassionate dialogue.

This also springs from the First Mindfulness Training. It is the spirit of free inquiry. I think Westerners can accept this, because you understand it. If you can find a way to organize it globally, it will be a happy event for the world.

Fourth: Aware that looking deeply at the nature of suffering can help us develop compassion and find ways out of suffering, we are determined not to avoid or close our eyes before suffering. We are committed to finding ways, including personal contact, images, and sounds, to be with those who suffer, so we can understand their situation deeply and help them transform their suffering into compassion, peace, and joy.

The first Dharma talk given by the Buddha was on the Four Noble Truths. The first truth is the existence of suffering. Contact with and awareness of suffering is needed. If we don't encounter pain, ills, we won't look for the causes of pain and ills to find a remedy, a way out of the situation.

America is somehow a closed society. Americans are not very aware of what is going on outside of America. Life here is so busy that even if you watch television and read the newspaper, and the images from outside flash by, there is no real contact. I hope you will find some way to nourish the awareness of the existence of suffering in the world. Of course, inside America there is also suffering, and it is important to stay in touch with that. But much of the suffering in the West is unnecessary and can vanish when we see the real suffering of other people. Sometimes we suffer because of some psychological fact. We cannot get out of our self, and so we suffer. If we get in touch with the suffering in the world and are moved by that suffering, we may come forward to help the people who are suffering, and our own suffering may just vanish.

Fifth: Aware that true happiness is rooted in peace, solidity, freedom, and compassion, and not in wealth or fame, we are determined not to take as the aim of our life fame, profit, wealth, or sensual pleasure, nor to accumulate wealth while millions are hungry and dying. We are committed to living simply and sharing our time, energy, and material resources with those in need. We will practice mindful consuming, not using alcohol, drugs, or any other products that bring toxins into our own and the collective body and consciousness.

The *Eight Realizations of Great Beings Sutra* says, "The human mind is always searching for possessions, and never feels fulfilled. Bodhisattvas move in the opposite direction and follow the principle of self-sufficiency. They live a simple life in order to practice the Way, and consider the realization of perfect understanding as their only career." In the context of our modern society, simple living also means to remain as free as possible from the destructive social and economic machine, and to avoid stress, depression, high blood pressure, and other modern diseases. We should make every effort to avoid the pressures and anxieties that fill most modern lives. The only way out is to consume less. Once we are able to live simply and happily, we are better able to help others.

Sixth: Aware that anger blocks communication and creates suffering, we are determined to take care of the energy of anger when it arises and to recognize and transform the seeds of anger that lie deep in our consciousness. When anger comes up, we are determined not to do or say anything, but to practice mindful breathing or mindful walking and acknowledge, embrace, and look deeply into our anger. We will learn to look with the eyes of compassion at those we think are the cause of our anger.

We have to be aware of irritation or anger as it arises, and try to understand it. Once we understand, we are better able to forgive and love. Meditation on compassion means meditation on understanding. If we do not understand, we cannot love.

"Learn to look at other beings with the eyes of compassion" is a quote from the *Lotus Sutra* chapter on Avalokiteshvara. You might like to write this down and put it in your sitting room. The original Chinese is only five words: "compassionate eyes looking living beings." The first time I recited the *Lotus Sutra*, when I came to these five words, I was silenced. I knew that these five words are enough to guide my whole life.

Seventh: Aware that life is available only in the present moment and that it is possible to live happily in the here and now, we are committed to training ourselves to live deeply each moment of daily life. We will try not to lose ourselves in dispersion or be carried away by regrets about the past, worries about the future, or craving, anger, or jealousy in the present. We will practice mindful breathing to come back to what is happening in the present moment. We are determined to learn the art of mindful living by touching the wondrous, refreshing, and healing elements that are inside and around us, and by nourishing seeds of joy, peace, love, and understanding in ourselves, thus facilitating the work of transformation and healing in our consciousness.

This mindfulness training is in the middle. It is the heart of the Fourteen Mindfulness Trainings, the most important one: to live in awareness. Without this training, without mindfulness, the other mindfulness trainings cannot be observed completely. It is like a carrying pole. In Asia they used to carry things with a pole, and put the middle of the pole on their shoulders. This training is like the middle of the pole that you carry on your shoulders.

Eighth: Aware that lack of communication always brings separation and suffering, we are committed to training ourselves in the practice of compassionate listening and loving speech. We will learn to listen deeply without judging or reacting and refrain from uttering words that can create discord or cause the community to break. We will make every effort to keep communications open and to reconcile and resolve all conflicts, however small.

We now come to the second set of mindfulness trainings, concerning speech. The first seven trainings deal with mind, then two with speech, and five with body. This mindfulness training is about reconciliation, the effort to make peace, not only in your family, but in society as well. In order to help reconcile a conflict, we have to be in touch with both sides. We must transcend the conflict; if we are still in the conflict, it is difficult to reconcile. We have to have a non-dualistic viewpoint in order to listen to both sides and understand. The world needs people like this for the work of reconciliation, people with the capacity of understanding and compassion.

Ninth: Aware that words can create suffering or happiness, we are committed to learning to speak truthfully and constructively, using only words that inspire hope and confidence. We are determined not to say untruthful things for the sake of personal interest or to impress people, nor to utter words that might cause division or hatred. We will not spread news that we do not know to be certain nor criticize or condemn things of which we are not sure. We will do our best to speak out about situations of injustice, even when doing so may threaten our safety.

The words we speak can create love, trust, and happiness around us, or create a hell. We should be careful about what we say. If we tend to talk too much, we should become aware of it and learn to speak less. We must become aware of our speech and the results of our speaking. There is a gatha that can be recited before picking up the telephone:

> Words can travel across thousands of miles.
> May my words create mutual understanding
>   and love.
> May they be as beautiful as gems,
> as lovely as flowers.

We should speak constructively. In our speech we can try not to cause misunderstanding, hatred, or jealousy, rather to increase understanding and mutual acceptance. This may even help reduce our telephone bills. The Ninth Mindfulness Training also requires frankness and courage. How many of us are brave enough to denounce injustice in a situation in which speaking the truth might threaten our own safety?

Tenth: Aware that the essence and aim of a Sangha is the practice of understanding and compassion, we are determined not to use the Buddhist community for personal gain or profit or transform our community into a political instrument. A spiritual community should, however, take a clear stand against oppression and injustice and should strive to change the situation without engaging in partisan conflicts.

This does not mean that we must be silent about injustice. It just means we should do it with awareness and not take sides. We should speak the truth and not just weigh the political consequences. If we take sides, we will lose our power to help mediate the conflict.

During one visit to America, I met with a group of people who wanted to raise funds to help the government of Vietnam rebuild the country. I asked whether they would also like to do something for the boat people, and they said no. They thought that politically it is not good to talk about the boat people, because that would discredit the government of Vietnam. In order to succeed in one thing, they have to refrain from doing something that they think is right.

Eleventh: Aware that great violence and injustice have been done to our environment and society, we are committed not to live with a vocation that is harmful to humans and nature. We will do our best to select a livelihood that helps realize our ideal of understanding and compassion. Aware of global economic, political, and social realities, we will behave responsibly as consumers and as citizens, not investing in companies that deprive others of their chance to live.

This is an extremely hard training to observe. If you are lucky enough to have a vocation that helps you realize your ideal of compassion, you still have to understand more deeply. If I am a teacher, I am very glad to have this job helping children. I am glad that I am not a butcher who kills cows and pigs. Yet the son and the daughter of the butcher come to my class, and I teach them. They profit from my right livelihood. My son and daughter eat the meat that the butcher prepares. We are linked together. I cannot say that my livelihood is perfectly right. It cannot be. Observing this mindfulness training includes finding ways to realize a collective right livelihood.

You may try to follow a vegetarian diet, to lessen the killing of animals, but you cannot completely avoid the killing. When you drink a glass of water, you kill many tiny living beings. Even in your dish of vegetables, there are quite a lot of them, boiled or fried. I am aware that my vegetarian dish is not completely vegetarian, and I think that if my teacher, the Buddha, were here, he could not avoid that either. The problem is whether we are determined to go in the direction of compassion or not. If we are, then can we reduce the suffering to a minimum? If I lose my direction, I have to look for the North Star, and I go to the north. That does not mean I expect to arrive at the North Star. I just want to go in that direction.

Twelfth: Aware that much suffering is caused by war and conflict, we are determined to cultivate nonviolence, under-standing, and compassion in our daily lives, to promote peace education, mindful mediation, and reconciliation within fam-ilies, communities, nations, and in the world. We are deter-mined not to kill and not to let others kill. We will diligently practice deep looking with our Sangha to discover better ways to protect life and prevent war.

The defense budgets in Western countries are still enor-mous. Studies show that by stopping the arms race, we will have more than enough money to erase poverty, hunger, illiteracy, and many diseases from the world.

This mindfulness training applies not only to humans, but to all living beings. As we have seen, no one can observe this training to perfection; however, the essence is to respect and protect life, to do our best to protect life. This means not killing, and also not letting other people kill. It is difficult. Those who try to observe this training have to be working for peace in order to have peace in themselves. Preventing war is much better than protesting against the war. Protesting the war is too late.

Thirteenth: Aware of the suffering caused by exploitation, social injustice, stealing, and oppression, we are committed to cultivating loving kindness and learning ways to work for the well-being of people, animals, plants, and minerals. We will practice generosity by sharing our time, energy, and material resources with those who are in need. We are determined not to steal and not to possess anything that should belong to others. We will respect the property of others, but will try to prevent others from profiting from human suffering or the suffering of other beings.

Bringing to our awareness the pain caused by social injustice, the Thirteenth Mindfulness Training urges us to work for a more livable society. This training is linked with the Fourth Mindfulness Training (the awareness of suffering), the Fifth Mindfulness Training (lifestyle), the Eleventh Mindfulness Training (right livelihood), and the Twelfth Mindfulness Training (the protection of life). In order to deeply comprehend this training, we must also meditate on these four mindfulness trainings.

To develop ways to prevent others from profiting from human suffering and the suffering of other beings is the duty of legislators and politicians. However, each of us can also act in this direction. To some degree, we can be close to oppressed people and help them protect their right to life and defend themselves against oppression and exploitation. Letting people profit from human suffering or the suffering of other beings is something we cannot do. As a community we must try to prevent this. How to work for justice in our own city is a problem we have to consider. The bodhisattvas' vows—to help all sentient beings—are immense. Each of us can vow to sit in their rescue boats.

Fourteenth: (For lay members): Aware that sexual relations motivated by craving cannot dissipate the feeling of loneliness but will create more suffering, frustration, and isolation, we are determined not to engage in sexual relations without mutual understanding, love, and a long-term commitment. In sexual relations, we must be aware of future suffering that may be caused. We know that to preserve the happiness of ourselves and others, we must respect the rights and commitments of ourselves and others. We will do everything in our power to protect children from sexual abuse and to protect couples and families from being broken by sexual misconduct. We will treat our bodies with respect and preserve our vital energies (sexual, breath, spirit) for the realization of our bodhisattva ideal. We will be fully aware of the responsibility of bringing new lives into the world, and will meditate on the world into which we are bringing new beings.

(For monastic members): Aware that the aspiration of a monk or a nun can only be realized when he or she wholly leaves behind the bonds of worldly love, we are committed to practicing chastity and to helping others protect themselves. We are aware that loneliness and suffering cannot be alleviated by the coming together of two bodies in a sexual relationship, but by the practice of true understanding and compassion. We know that a sexual relationship will destroy our life as a monk or a nun, will prevent us from realizing our ideal of serving living beings, and will harm others. We are determined not to suppress or mistreat our body or to look upon our body as only an instrument, but to learn to handle our body with respect. We are determined to preserve vital energies (sexual, breath, spirit) for the realization of our bodhisattva ideal.

You may have the impression that this mindfulness training discourages having children, but it is not so. It only urges us to be aware of what we are doing. Is our world safe enough to bring in more children? If you want to bring more children into the world, then do something for the world.

This training also has to do with celibacy. Traditionally, Buddhist monks were celibate for at least three reasons. The first is that the monks in the time of the Buddha were urged to practice meditation for most of the day. They had to be in contact with the people in the village in order to teach them the Dharma, and in order to ask for some food for the day. If a monk had to support a family, he would not be able to perform his duties as a monk.

The second reason is that sexual energy had to be preserved for meditation. In the religious and medical traditions of Asia, the human person was said to have three sources of energy: sexual, breath, and spirit. Sexual energy is what you spend during sexual intercourse. Breath energy is the kind of energy you spend when you talk too much and breathe too little. Spirit energy is energy that you spend when you worry too much and do not sleep well. If you spend these three sources of energy, your body will not be strong enough to penetrate deeply into reality and realize the Way. Buddhist monks observed celibacy, not because of moral admonition, but to conserve energy. Someone on a long fast knows how important it is to preserve these three sources of energy.

The third reason Buddhist monks observed celibacy is the question of suffering. Even today, if we go to India we see many children without food and many children sick without medicine. One woman can give birth to ten, twelve children, without being able to feed two or three properly. The existence of suffering is the first truth in Buddhism. To bring a child into the world is a great responsibility. If you are wealthy, maybe you can do it with no problem. But if you are poor, this is a real concern. To be reborn means first to be reborn in your children. Your children are a continuation of yourself. You are reborn in them, and you continue the cycle of suffering. Aware that having more children in the society of his day would be to make them suffer, the Buddha urged the monks not to have children. I think that during the past 2,500 years,

Buddhist monks in many countries have helped curb the birth rate. That is quite important.

The Fourteenth Mindfulness Training urges us to respect our own body and to maintain our energy for the realization of the Way. Not only meditation, but any efforts that are required to change the world require energy. We should take good care of ourselves.

In my opinion, the liberation of sexual behavior in the West has caused a number of good results, but has also caused some problems. The liberation of women, because of modern birth control methods, has been something very real. In the past, young girls in Asia as well as Europe had enormous problems and some even committed suicide when they became pregnant. Since the discovery of birth control, these kinds of tragedies have lessened considerably. But the liberation of sexual behavior has also caused much stress, much trouble. I think the fact that many people suffer from depression is partly because of that. Please meditate on this problem. It is an important problem for Western society.

If you wish to have children, please do something for the world you will bring them into. That will make you someone who works for peace, in one way or another.

Meditation in Daily Life

*D*uring retreats, from time to time a Bell Master invites the bell to sound, silently reciting this poem first:

> Body, speech, and mind in perfect oneness,
> I send my heart along with the sound of the bell.
> May the hearer awaken from forgetfulness
> And transcend all anxiety and sorrow.

Then he or she breathes three times, and invites the bell to sound. When the rest of us hear the bell, we stop our thinking and breathe in and out three times, reciting this verse:

> Listen, listen,
> This wonderful sound
> brings me back to my true self.

Meditation is to be aware of what is going on: in your body, in your feelings, in your mind, and in the world. The most precious practice in Buddhism is meditation, and it is important to practice meditation in a joyful mood. We have to smile a lot in order to be able to meditate. The Bell of Mindfulness helps us to do this.

*   *   *

Suppose we have a son who becomes an unbearable young man. It may be hard for us to love him. That is natural. In order to be loved, a person should be lovable. If our son has become difficult to love, we will be very unhappy. We wish we could love him, but the only way we can is to understand him, to understand his situation. We have to take our son as the subject of our meditation. Instead of taking the concept of emptiness or some other subject, we can take our son as a concrete subject for our meditation.

First we need to stop the invasion of feelings and thoughts, which deplete our strength in meditation, and cultivate the capacity, the power of concentration. In Sanskrit this is called *samadhi*. For a child to do his homework he has to stop chewing gum and stop listening to the radio, so he can concentrate on the homework. If we want to understand our son, we have to learn to stop the things that divert our attention. Concentration, samadhi, is the first practice of meditation.

When we have a light bulb, for the light to concentrate on our book, we need a lamp shade to keep the light from dispersing, to concentrate the light so that we can read the book more easily. The practice of concentration is like acquiring a lamp shade to help us concentrate our mind on something. While doing sitting or walking meditation, cutting the future, cutting the past, dwelling in the present time, we develop our own power of concentration. With that power of concentration, we can look deeply into the problem. This is insight meditation. First we are aware of the problem, focusing all our attention on the problem, and then we look deeply into it in order to understand its real nature, in this case the nature of our son's unhappiness.

We don't blame our son. We just want to understand why he has become like that. Through this method of meditation, we find out all the causes, near and far, that have led to our son's present state of being. The more we see, the more we understand. The more we understand, the easier it is for us to have compassion and love. Understanding is the source of love. Understanding is love itself. Understanding is another name for love; love is another name for understanding. When we practice Buddhism, it is helpful to practice in this way.

When you grow a tree, if it does not grow well, you don't blame the tree. You look into the reasons it is not doing well. You may need fertilizer, or more water, or less sun. You never blame the tree, yet we blame our son. If we know how to take care of him, he will grow well, like a tree. Blaming has no effect at all. Never blame, never try to persuade using reason and arguments. They never lead to any positive effect. That is my experience. No argument, no reasoning, no blame, just understanding. If you understand, and you show that you understand, you can love, and the situation will change.

*   *   *

The Bell of Mindfulness is the voice of the Buddha calling us back to ourselves. We have to respect that sound, stop our thinking and talking, and go back to ourselves, with a smile and breathing. It is not a Buddha from the outside. It is our own Buddha who calls us. If we cannot hear the sound of the bell, then we cannot hear other sounds which also come from the Buddha, like the sound of the wind, the sound of the bird, even the sounds of cars or a baby crying. They are all a call from the Buddha to return to ourselves. Practicing with a bell from time to time is helpful, and once you can practice with a bell, you can practice with the wind and other sounds. After that you can practice not only with the sounds, but with forms. The sunlight coming through your window is also a calling from Dharmakaya in order for the Buddhakaya to be, and also for the Sanghakaya to be real.

"Calming, Smiling, Present moment, Wonderful moment." While you sit you can recite that, and while you do walking meditation you can use that, or you can use other methods, like counting: Breathing in, one. Breathing out, one. Breathing in, two. Out, two.

In, three; out, three. Until ten, and then you decrease: ten, and then nine, eight, seven. Counting the breath is one of the ways to educate yourself for concentration, samadhi.

If you do not have enough concentration, you cannot be strong enough to break through, to have a breakthrough into a subject of your meditation. Therefore breathing, walking, sitting, and other practices are primarily for you to realize some degree of concentration. This is called *Stop*. Stop, in order to concentrate. Just as the lamp shade stops the light from dispersing so you can read your book more easily, the first step of meditation is stopping, stopping the dispersion, concentrating on one subject. The best subject, the most available subject, is your breathing. Breathing is wonderful. It unites body and mind. Whether you count breaths or just follow them, it is for stopping.

Stopping and seeing are very close. As soon as you stop, the words on the page become clear, the problem of our son becomes clear. Stop and look, that's meditation, insight meditation. Insight means you have a vision, an insight into reality. Stopping is also to see, and seeing helps to stop. The two are one. We do so much, we run so quickly, the situation is difficult, and many people say, "Don't just sit there, do something." But doing more things may make the situation worse. So you should say, "Don't just do something, sit there." Sit there, stop, be yourself first, and begin from there. That is the meaning of meditation. When you sit in the meditation hall or at home or wherever you are, you can do that. But you have to really sit. Just sitting is not enough. Sit and be. Sitting without being is not sitting. Be stopping and seeing.

There are so many methods of stopping and seeing, and intelligent teachers will be able to invent ways to help you. In Buddhism it is said that there are 84,000 Dharma doors for you to enter reality. Dharma doors are means of practice, ways of practice. When we ride on a horse that is out of control, I think our deepest wish is to stop. How can we stop? We have to resist the speed, the losing of ourselves, and therefore we must organize a resistance. Spending two hours on one cup of tea during a tea meditation is an act of resistance, nonviolent resistance. We can do it because we have a Sanghakaya. We can do it together, we can resist a way of life that makes us lose ourselves. Walking meditation is also resistance. Sitting is also resistance. So if you want to stop the course of armaments, you have to resist, and begin by resisting in your own daily life. I saw a car from New York with a bumper sticker, "Let peace begin with me." That's correct. And let me begin with peace. That is also correct.

*　　*　　*

Walking meditation can be very enjoyable. We walk slowly, alone or with friends, if possible in some beautiful place. Walking meditation is really to enjoy the walking. Walking not in order to arrive, just for walking. The purpose is to be in the present moment and enjoy each step you make. Therefore you have to shake off all worries and anxieties, not thinking of the future, not thinking of the past, just enjoying the present moment. You can take the hand of a child as you do it. You walk, you make steps as if you are the happiest person on Earth.

We walk all the time, but usually it is more like running. When we walk like that, we print anxiety and sorrow on the Earth. We have to walk in a way that we only print peace and serenity on Earth. Every one of us can do that provided that we want it very much. Any child can do that. If we can take one step like that, we can take two, three, four, and five. When we are able to take one step peacefully, happily, we are for the cause of peace and happiness for the whole of humankind. Walking meditation is a wonderful practice.

*   *   *

The Buddha's basic Dharma talk concerning meditation, the *Satipatthana Sutta*, is available in Pali, Chinese, and many other languages, including English and French. According to this text, to meditate is to be aware of what is going on in your body, in your feelings, in your mind, and in the objects of your mind, which are the world. If you are aware of what is going on, then you can see problems as they unfold, and you can help prevent many of them. When things explode, it is too late. How we deal with our daily lives is the most important question.

How we deal with our feelings, our speaking, with
ordinary things every day is just meditation. We
must learn to apply meditation in our daily lives.

There are many easy things to do. For instance,
before eating the evening meal, everyone can sit
around the table, and practice breathing, three slow
breaths. You breathe to recover yourself, to be yourself. I am sure that every time you breathe deeply like
that, you become entirely yourself again. Then before
eating you can look at everyone and smile, just two
or three seconds, not much, for each person. We
never have time to look at each other, even those we
love, and soon it will be too late. It is wonderful to do
that, to openly appreciate everyone in our own
household.

In Plum Village, it is a child who reads the gatha
before eating. Holding up a bowl of rice, he knows he
is very lucky. Being a refugee he knows that in many
countries of Southeast Asia, children do not have
enough to eat. The kind of rice that they buy in the
West is the best kind of rice imported from Thailand.
The children know that even in Thailand, Thai children do not have the opportunity to eat such rice.
They eat poorer quality rice. The good rice is
exported for the country to get foreign currency.
When a refugee boy holds up a bowl of rice, he has to
remember that he is lucky. He knows that 40,000 children his age die in the world each day because of
hunger. Then the child says something like this:
"Today, on the table there are good things that Mama
just cooked. There I see Papa, there I see my brother,

there I see my sister; it is so good to be together and eat together like this, while there are many who are hungry. I feel very thankful."

There are so many practices we can do to bring awareness into our everyday lives: breathing between telephone calls, walking meditation between business meetings, practicing meditation while helping hungry children or war victims. Buddhism must be engaged. What is the use of practicing meditation if it does not have anything to do with our daily lives?

*   *   *

You can feel very happy while practicing breathing and smiling. The conditions are available. You can do it in a meditation hall. You can do it at home. You can do it in a park, along the riverside, anywhere. I would like to suggest that in each home we have a tiny room for breathing. We have a room for sleeping, a room for eating, and a room for cooking, why not have one room for breathing? Breathing is very important.

I suggest that that room be decorated very simply, and not be too bright. You may want to have a small bell, one with a beautiful sound, a few cushions or chairs, and perhaps a pot of flowers to remind us of our true nature. Children can arrange flowers in mindfulness, smiling. If your household has five members, you can have five cushions or chairs, plus a few for guests. From time to time, you might like to invite a guest to come and sit and breathe with you for five minutes, or three minutes.

If you want to have a statue or a painting of a Buddha, please be choosy. Many times I see Buddhas who are not relaxed and peaceful. The artists who make them do not practice breathing, smiling. Be choosy if you ask a Buddha to come home. A Buddha should be smiling, happy, beautiful, for the sake of our children. If they look at the Buddha and don't feel refreshed and happy, then it is not a good statue. If you don't find a beautiful Buddha, wait, and have a flower instead. A flower is a Buddha. A flower has Buddha nature.

I know of families where children go into a room like that after breakfast, sit down and breathe for ten times, in-out-one, in-out-two, in-out-three, ten times, and then they go to school. This is a very beautiful practice. If your child doesn't wish to breathe ten times, how about three times? Beginning the day with being a Buddha is a very nice way to start the day. If we are a Buddha in the morning and we try to nourish the Buddha throughout the day, we may be able to come home at the end of a day with a smile— the Buddha is still there.

When you become agitated, you do not have to do or say anything. Just follow your breathing and walk slowly into that room. (The room for breathing also symbolizes our own inner Buddha Land, so we can enter it whenever we need to, even if we are not at home). I have a friend who, whenever he becomes agitated, enters the breathing room in his home. He sits down respectfully, breathes in and out three times, invites the bell to sound, and recites the gatha.

Immediately he feels better. If he needs to sit longer, he stays there. From time to time, his wife hears the sound of the bell, and it reminds her to be mindful in her work. At such times, she deeply appreciates her husband. "He is so wonderful, quite different from others. He knows how to deal with anger." If she has been irritated, her own resentment subsides. Sometimes she stops what she is doing and goes into the breathing room to sit with him. This picture is so lovely, more beautiful than an expensive painting. Doing things in this way has a good effect on everyone, teaching by example, not just with words. When your child is agitated, you don't have to say, "Go to that room!" You can take his or her hand and walk together into the room for breathing, and sit quietly together. This is the best education for peace.

It is really beautiful to begin the day by being a Buddha. Each time we feel ourselves about to leave our Buddha, we can sit and breathe until we return to our true self. There are three things I can recommend to you: arranging to have a breathing room in your home, a room for meditation; practicing breathing, sitting, for a few minutes every morning at home with your children; and going out for a slow walking meditation with your children before going to sleep, just ten minutes is enough. These things are very important. They can change our civilization.

About the author

Thich Nhat Hanh was born in central Vietnam in 1926, and he left home as a teenager to become a Zen monk. He founded the School of Youth for Social Service, Van Hanh Buddhist University, and the Order of Interbeing. In 1966, he was invited by the Fellowship of Reconciliation to tour the United States to describe to us the enormous suffering of his people. Because of his fierce neutrality, he was unable to return home, and he was granted asylum in France, where he is head of a small community of meditators and activists. Thich Nhat Hanh is author of many books, including *Living Buddha, Living Christ, Peace Is Every Step,* and *Old Path White Clouds.*

About the illustrator

Born in a suburb of Tokyo in 1941, Mayumi Oda shares Thich Nhat Hanh's understanding of the sufferings of war, coupled with a passionate commitment to the expression of joy. An internationally recognized artist, her bold contemporary imagery has been identified with the work of Matisse. She has had many one-woman exhibits in Japan and the U.S., and her work is in the permanent collections of the Museum of Modern Art in New York, the Museum of Fine Arts in Boston, and the Library of Congress. Mayumi Oda now lives and works near the Green Gulch Zen Center, just north of San Francisco.

About the editor

Arnold Kotler was an ordained student at the San Francisco and Tassajara Zen Centers from 1969 to 1984. He is the founding editor of Parallax Press and a member of Thich Nhat Hanh's Order of Interbeing.

Parallax Press publishes books on engaged Buddhism and the practice of mindfulness by Thich Nhat Hanh and other authors. All of Thich Nhat Hanh's work is available at our on-line store and in our free catalog. For a copy of the catalog, please contact:

Parallax Press
P.O. Box 7355
Berkeley, CA 94707
www.parallax.org
Tel: 510 525-0101

Monastics and lay people practice the art of mindful living in the tradition of Thich Nhat Hanh at retreat communities in France and the United States. Individuals, couples, and families are invited to join these communities for a Day of Mindfulness and longer practice periods. For information, please visit www.plumvillage.org or contact:

Plum Village
13 Martineau
33580 Dieulivol, France
info@plumvillage.org

Green Mountain Dharma Center
P.O. Box 182
Hartland Four Corners, VT 05049
mfmaster@vermontel.net
Tel: 802 436-1103

Deer Park Monastery
2499 Melru Lane
Escondido, CA 92026
deerpark@plumvillage.org
Tel: 760 291-1003